THE ORIGINAL SCOTCH

November 6. 1865.

The District of Glenlivet, a part of the Gordon property in Scotland belongs to me

My tenants George and John Gordon Smith, whose distillery of malt Whiskey is called "The Glenlivet" "Distillery" - are the only distillers in the Glenlivet district ~

Richmond.

The Original Scotch

A HISTORY OF SCOTCH WHISKY

FROM THE EARLIEST DAYS

BY MICHAEL BRANDER

HUTCHINSON OF LONDON

HUTCHINSON & CO (Publishers) LTD
3 Fitzroy Square, London W1

London Melbourne Sydney Auckland
Wellington Johannesburg Cape Town
and agencies throughout the world

First published 1974
© Michael Brander 1974

Designed and produced by Hutchinson Benham Limited
Set in Monotype Walbaum
Printed and bound in Great Britain by W & J Mackay Limited
Chatham

ISBN 0 09 120720 7

To

OSKAR KOKOSCHKA
THE GREAT ARTIST
Whom I introduced to The Original Scotch

JOSEPH HISLOP
THE GREAT TENOR
Who being Scots needed no introduction

&

BILL SMITH GRANT
ANOTHER GENIUS
Who distils it

Contents

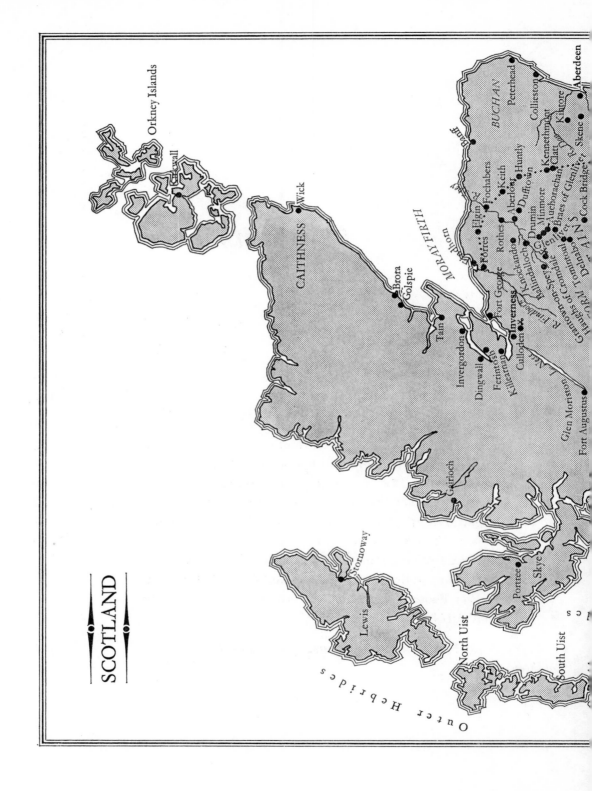

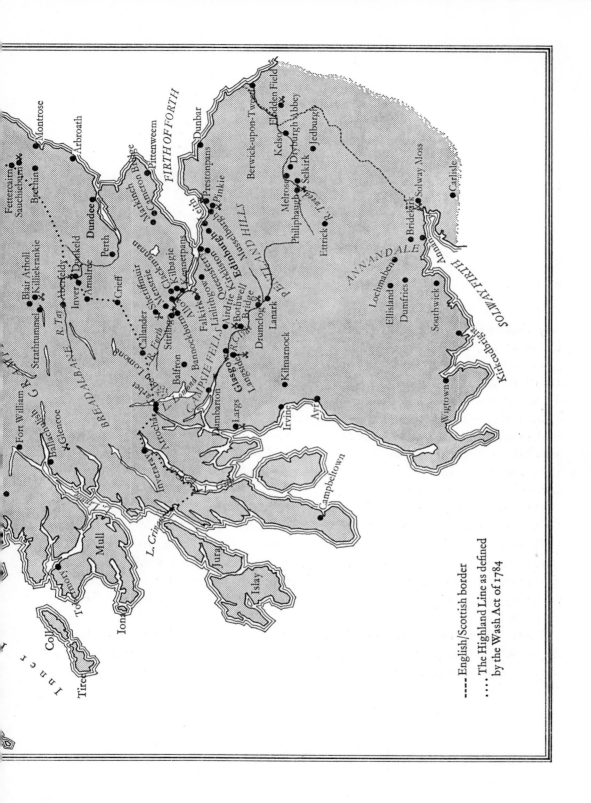

Acknowledgements

My thanks are due to many people, whisky distillers and others connected with the industry, for their ready help and advice while writing this book. For their generous hospitality as well as assistance in the background research I must first thank Captain W. H. and Mrs. Smith Grant. My thanks are also due to Major D. Mackessack and Mr. R. L. Grant, who patiently answered numerous queries. I must of course also thank The Glenlivet Distillers for their generous backing and for making me free of their archives. Also outstandingly patient and helpful was Mr. G. S. Grant of The Glenfarclas Distillery, but it is only fair to say that throughout the entire industry I found enormous willingness to help with this book in every way possible.

Outside the industry I would particularly like to thank Mr. W. J. Campbell, Collector, H.M. Customs & Excise, Edinburgh, and Mr. Walter Welch, Collector, H.M. Customs & Excise, Aberdeen. The Librarians and Staff of many libraries in Scotland were also of great assistance, but I would particularly like to express my indebtedness to the Staff of the National Library of Scotland in Edinburgh and to the late Mr. W. Leslie and Staff of the East Lothian Library.

Lastly I must thank all those, both inside and outside the industry, including my wife and family, who read and commented on the typescript and proofs. It only remains to add that for any errors of omission or commission I am entirely responsible.

List of Illustrations

BLACK-AND-WHITE PLATES

FIGURES IN THE TEXT

Drawings for the chapter headings by Chloë Furze

Author's Preface

My earliest contact with whisky in any quantity was at the age of three when I fell through a skylight which I had mistakenly thought would bear my weight. On the way to the floor some fifteen feet below I bounced providentially off a sideboard laden with whisky and sherry decanters adding the crash of crystal to that of glass. My nurse rushing unerringly to the sound found me sitting amid the wreckage soaked to the skin in a mixture of Speyside malts, blends and amontillado, sucking my thumb with a rather pleased expression on my face. I was found to be unhurt except for a minor gash and was packed off to a bath and bed to avoid the wrath of my father at the sacrilege I had unwittingly committed. Since then I have often felt that I did not appreciate the experience as fully as I might have done, for it is not everyone who has been outwardly soaked in whisky; but the Speyside malts, in particular The Glenlivet and Glen Grant, have remained my favourite whiskies.

That the former should be 'The Original Scotch' of the title is quite fortuitous, but it has added a certain pleasure to my researches into the growth of the Scotch Whisky industry. As a Scot with an early interest in Scotch whisky from the consumer's side, this has in any event been a pleasure and a source of interest rather than a chore. There is nothing quite like Scotch whisky, neat or with water, applied internally or externally. It remains the nearest the alchemists of old ever achieved to attaining the secret of eternal life for which they were always searching. 'Uisge beatha' or 'usquebaugh', the water of life, is the very produce of the air, water and soil of Scotland. It is the distilled essence of Scotland itself.

Introduction

This is a history of the development of Scotch whisky from the earliest days to the present time. It is therefore, of necessity, in part a history of the Scottish nation, for it is the Scots who have produced Scotch whisky and it is an essential and important part of the national life, the greatest export in Britain, the foremost industry in Scotland and the source of social conviviality at important Scots feasts such as Hogmanay. To understand how the Scotch whisky industry developed it is necessary to start at the beginning when Scotland and England were still warring nations. The effects of the Union of the Crowns and subsequent Act of Union, the economic consequences which flowed from them, the effects of penal taxation applied from the south on Scots, Scotland and Scotch whisky production all have to be examined in turn.

The Original Scotch of the title, the malt whisky, twice distilled in the time-honoured and unequalled fashion, was the whisky which first was licensed and accepted by Act of Parliament. The first licence taken out was that for The Glenlivet whisky by George Smith in 1824, one hundred and fifty years ago. By that time we may accept that whisky had been made in Scotland for eight hundred years at least, although the earliest record extant is dated 1494. It was only in 1830 that the Patent Coffey still was introduced which produced a straight grain whisky in one continuous distilling process. When the old straight malt and the Lowland grain whiskies were blended from 1853 onwards the steady growth of Scotch whisky as it is known today the whole world over first began. By the 1870s the first whisky boom was beginning. Since then it has been exported all round the world and millions other than merely expatriate Scots have come to appreciate Scotch whisky, with its unique flavour and purity. Now the wheel has come full circle once more and those of discrimination are demanding straight malt, the Original Scotch, rather than a blend, but straight or blended the product of Scotland remains unequalled elsewhere in the world.

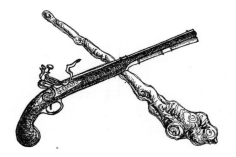

1. Origins of Distilling to James I & VI

From the bonny bells of heather
They brewed a drink long-syne,
Was sweeter far than honey,
Was stronger far than wine.

R. L. STEVENSON 1850–1894

The earliest and most primitive form of distillation was accomplished simply by heating fermented liquor over a fire in an enclosed vessel with a long spout. The alcohol having a lower boiling point than water vapourised first and rose in the form of steam which condensed in the spout as it cooled and dripped steadily into another container. The resultant mixture contained, amongst many impurities, pure alcohol. Even the most complex modern stills today are founded on this extremely simple basic principle.

The art of distillation originated in the Far East long before the birth of Christ. Age-old methods of distillation using gourds and hollow bamboo may still be seen in primitive areas of the East to this day. Indeed it may be that the availability of hollow tubes of bamboo contributed to the development of the process there initially. Certainly arrack is known to have been manufactured in India as far back as 800 B.C. It is also known that for over a thousand years previously spirits of one sort or another had been distilled in China and India.

The process seems to have reached Europe via the Ancient Egyptians, who practised distilling from about the 8th century B.C. As early as the 4th century B.C. Aristotle was familiar with the principles involved. A translation of his *Meteorology* reads: 'Sea water can be rendered drinkable by distillation; wine and other liquids can be subjected to the same process. After they have been converted into steam they return to liquids'. In Europe, however, with plentiful supplies of wine readily available, though the theory may have been known, the process does not seem to have been greatly practised at this early period.

Quite how, or when, the process reached Britain is now purely a matter for conjecture. Whether it was brought by the Phoenicians, those great seafaring merchants of the Mediterranean, or whether it came over with the Romans, cannot be told. One of the first references to distilling appears in the 6th-century *Mead Song* of the Welsh bard Taliessin, who sang:

> Mead distilled sparkling, its praise is everywhere.

He also composed a *Song to Ale*, indicating clearly a considerable familiarity with the methods of malting and brewing, the first stages prior to distilling spirits from grain. He wrote:

> He shall steep it in the Llyn
> Until it shall sprout.

The modern method of malting barley is to steep it in water for two or three days according to the type of barley, the time of year and the weather, then spread it on a stone floor up to a depth of two or three feet and allow it to germinate. The grain is then turned with wooden shovels as soon as the first roots begin to show and by the end of seven to eight days the bed is thinned out to about three or four inches deep. To distil malt whisky today it is then taken to be dried over peat smoke in a kiln, a refinement never envisaged by Taliessin, although the basic principles were clearly well enough understood. The *Song to Ale* continues:

> He shall steep it another time
> Until it is sodden.

The next stage in the modern process of distilling is to clean the dried malt of

2

rootlets and impurities, known as 'culms' or 'combings', and then crush it before mixing it with hot water in a 'mash tun'. The resulting mixture, known as 'wort', is cooled and then run off into a wooden container known as a 'wash back' and yeast is added to aid the fermentation. When fermentation starts the mixture is known as 'wash' and, once it is over, the 'wash' is ready for distillation.

The *Song to Ale* continued, perfectly correctly for the brewing of ale:

> Not for a long time will be finished
> What the elements produce.
> Let his vessels be washed,
> Let his wort be clear.
> And when there shall be an exciter of song,
> Let it be brought from the cell.

The importance of cleanliness in the whole process was apparently well understood even then, as was the desirability of keeping the product at an even temperature in a cellar. Since the art of distilling was also understood, it is clear that the Celts in Wales at this time also knew how to distil grain spirits. For how long they had possessed that knowledge can only be guessed.

According to legend it was St. Patrick, himself a native of Scotland, who taught the Irish the art of distilling, which would place it in the 5th century. In the same century the Scots from Ireland invaded the west of Scotland, dispossessing the native Picts, so that the knowledge may have passed either way and from them to the Welsh, or vice versa. It is only certain that when the English first invaded Ireland in the 12th century the inhabitants were manufacturing a spirit distilled from grain, and clearly the Scots also possessed the art by this time.

To understand how and why from these primitive beginnings the distilling of Scotch whisky eventually emerged as an occupation, an industry and an art peculiar to the Scots and Scotland it is necessary at this stage to glance briefly at the development of Scotland and the Scots nation. The clean air, the pure water and the peaty soil which contribute largely to the production of Scotch whisky as a unique national drink have changed but little, if at all, over the centuries. During the 13th and 14th centuries, however, the Scots had little time for peaceful pursuits such as distilling. Often at war amongst themselves, they were also embattled on two fronts. On the one hand they were beset by the Norwegians in the far north and the west and on the other by the English in the south. At one time or another Caithness, Orkney and the Western Isles were under Scandinavian domination and overlordship, while from the Lothians to the Tweed in the south there was what amounted to perennial war with England.

It was not until the battle of Largs in 1263 that the Norwegians suffered a major defeat and the Scandinavian hold on Scotland was loosened at last. Under the determined onslaughts of Edward I, 'the Hammer of the Scots', which followed, Scotland was welded at last into a united nation on the anvil of hatred. The reaction of the Scots under the leadership first of Wallace, then of Bruce, culminating in the decisive defeat of the English at Bannockburn in 1314 was defined by the famous Declaration of Arbroath: '. . . For as long as a hundred of us remain alive we are resolved never to submit to the domination of the English. It is not for glory, wealth or honour that we are fighting, but for freedom and freedom only, which no true man ever surrenders except with his life. . . .'

The spirit of profound hostility towards England, so clearly demonstrated by the Declaration of Arbroath, persisted for over three hundred years, until as late as the end of the 16th century, punctuated at intervals by open warfare between the two neighbouring nations. During the uneasy periods of peace exchanges of any sort between the two countries were few and guarded and Scottish trade was almost entirely directed towards the Netherlands and France. In the circumstances it is understandable that her natural ally should be France and that the 'auld alliance' should have considerable effect on Scotland's development in the ensuing centuries. Prior to the Reformation almost the only thing Scotland and England had in common was the same religion under the spiritual leadership of the Pope in Rome.

It was in the monastic calm of the abbeys or the monasteries that such pursuits as ale-making, wine-making and distilling reached their highest perfection, both in England and Scotland. Short of complete devastation in time of war, which was the fate of many fine Scots border abbeys, there was little likely to alter the even routine of monastic life. Almost invariably sited in rich agricultural land with continuity of tenure and few interruptions, it was natural enough that the monks should develop considerable expertise in agriculture, fruit-growing and associated skills. In England, for instance, the ale produced at the monastery near Burton on Trent was famous due to the special qualities of the water which contained magnesium salts and calcium sulphate, both necessary to brew good bitter ale.

It is not surprising therefore that the first record of distilling in Scotland should be found in an entry in the Exchequer Rolls for 1494, which reads: 'Eight bolls of malt to Friar John Cor, wherewith to make aqua vitae'. Since a boll amounts to ten stones, or 140 lbs, it is clear at once that this was no small operation. Half a ton of malt producing probably in the region of seventy gallons of spirit was not required purely for private consumption. Obviously the monastic establishment to which Friar John Cor was attached was distilling on no mean scale and the assumption that it was for the use of the royal court is not unreasonable.

At this stage the term aqua vitae, or water of life, was applied indiscriminately to any alcoholic liquid produced by distillation. The method of distilling wine, mentioned by Aristotle, was claimed as a fresh discovery by Albucasis, famed alchemist and physician of Cordova in Spain in the 9th century. Thereafter the production of a primitive form of brandy by this means was the jealously guarded secret of alchemists and religious houses in Europe. The aqua vitae produced from grain, specifically barley, in Scotland was in effect a primitive form of malt whisky. To be made drinkable each had to be mixed with herbs, essences or other liquors, except when used as a medicine a few drops at a time.

Further mention of aqua vitae begins to appear in official records at fairly frequent intervals after the first reference to Friar John Cor. For instance in 1498, in the Lord High Treasurer's Accounts, there is an entry reading: 'To the barbour that brocht aqua vitae to the King in Dundee be the Kingis command – ix s'. In this instance at least there was no doubt as to its destination. Aqua vitae was regarded as worthy of a king and to judge by other entries James IV was beginning to acquire a taste for it.

James IV had succeeded to the throne at the age of 18 on the assassination of his father after the battle of Sauchieburn in 1488. Within two decades he had accomplished more than his vacillating parent would ever have been likely to achieve. He had made Edinburgh the capital city, pacified the Highlands, and encouraged the rule of law, the arts and learning, including alchemy. No doubt in Scotland, as on the Continent, it was the alchemists seeking the elixir of eternal life who by constant experiment improved on the age-old methods of distillation, but generally, like the religious houses, they guarded their secrets jealously. Aqua vitae might be drunk by royalty and the nobility but it was not yet by any means the drink of the people.

With, or without, aqua vitae, however, it was a drunken age. The nobility might drink wine from France, but the mass of the nation drank ale, in vast quantities. William Dunbar, the poet of the day, wrote in *The Dance of the Sevin Deidle Synnis:*

> Than the foul monster Gluttony . . .
> Him followit mony foul drunkart,
> With can and collep, cop and quart,
> In surfeit and excess. . . .'

Close association with France over the centuries in accord with the 'auld alliance' had led to more than a liking for claret amongst the nobility, although this was a taste which lingered among wealthy Scots until well into the 19th century. It had led to the development of the Firth of Forth ports as important merchant centres dealing directly with the Continent. Scots wool, herring and salmon, pearls and oysters, then prevalent in the Forth, barrels of ale and quantities of coal were sent to France in small merchant ships. Silks and velvets, wine, both burgundy and claret, were amongst the goods imported in return. French cooking and even French architecture to a greater or lesser degree were adopted also, so that even today many Lowland Scots towns with their broad market places bear a resemblance to their French or Flemish counterparts.

Although it was by no means obvious at the time, however, James IV took the decisive step which was to end in union with England. After agreeing to a 'Treaty of Perpetual Peace' with England in 1502, he cemented this by marrying Henry VII's daughter Margaret Tudor in 1503. It may have been thanks to the 'auld alliance' that the fountains ran with wine at their wedding, but the future lay in union with England not with France. In exactly a hundred years the Union of the Crowns was to follow.

Meanwhile, in 1505, it is noteworthy that James granted the barber surgeons in Edinburgh the monopoly of distilling and selling aqua vitae within the capital, which right they seem to have exercised for the next fifty years at least. Notable also were two entries in the Lord High Treasurer's Accounts while James was in Inverness in 1506. On the 15th of September there is an entry: 'For aqua vite to the King – iii s.', and on the 17th: 'For ane flacet of aqua vite to the king – v s.'. By this time there can be little doubt that James drank it regularly.

Unfortunately when Henry VIII invaded France in 1513 James felt bound to make a counter-invasion of England to aid the 'auld ally', thus ending the 'perpetual peace'. He met an English army at Flodden and his leadership proved that he had more than his share of the impetuosity and boldness inherent in the Scots character. He was killed along with the flower of the Scots nobility and manhood in a totally mistimed and tactically indefensible attack. He was succeeded by his son, James V, aged 18 months.

Throughout the rest of Henry VIII's reign, until 1547, the Scots were subjected to periodic invasion and the ravaging of border towns, abbeys and villages. Jedburgh and Kelso were burned in 1523 and yet again in 1542. On James V's early death in 1542, soon after his own unsuccessful counter-invasion had been defeated at Solway Moss in the Borders, he was succeeded by his infant daughter Mary. In a determined effort to secure the Scots throne by marriage of the infant Mary to his son Edward, Henry pursued the policy known as the 'rough wooing'. He sent an army into Scotland and burned Edinburgh and Leith in 1544. The following year the English burned Dryburgh, Melrose and Kelso. Even after Henry's death in 1547 the English invaded yet again and defeated the Scots at Musselburgh Fields (or Pinkie). Apart from enhancing Scots hatred and distrust the policy had little effect, since Mary was in France soon to be betrothed to the Dauphin.

Despite Henry VIII's heavy-handed, obsessive efforts to gain the Scots throne by force, which merely ensured the dominance of the French Catholic party under Mary of Guise, James's widow, as regent, events favoured the union with England. The Reformation of the Church and the dissolution of the monasteries in England in 1539 were to have their echoes in Scotland within a decade. By 1560 Mary of Guise and her supporters had been overthrown and the Scottish Parliament had repudiated Roman Catholicism. The Kirk henceforth was to have a considerable hand in Scots affairs, indeed at times a great deal too much.

Meanwhile considerable advances were being made in the art of distillation. The first book on the subject in English, *The vertuose boke of Distyllacyon* by Hieronymous Braunschweig was published in 1527, translated by L. Andrew. The obvious Scottish origins of the translator are of interest as it seems likely that Scotland was still well to the fore in distilling. According to this book aqua vitae was regarded as purely medicinal and distillation was defined as: 'Distylling is none other thynge, but onely a puryfyeng of the grosse from the subtyll and the subtyll from the grosse'.

Following the Reformation and the dissolution of the monasteries in both England and Scotland numerous monks were forced to find trades for themselves, utilising the only skills they knew. Many became brewers, distillers, alchemists and doctors, with the result that there was a further spread in knowledge of distilling methods as the various skills and secrets which had previously been confined to a limited circle were spread over a much wider area. It is certainly obvious that as the 16th century progressed a much wider knowledge of distilling was to be found.

In 1559 the *Treasure of Evonymous* was published by Peter Morwyng giving greater details of the distilling process. His view was that it made no difference whether aqua vitae was distilled from good or bad wine, or even the lees of wine, but that: 'if it be distilled often it shal be made the more effectuall, hotter and drier'. He went on to extol its merits shamelessly as follows:

It helpeth red and duskish eyes. It is good for them that have the falling sickness if they drink it. It cureth the palsy if they be onoynted therewith. It sharpeneth the wit, it restoreth memori. It maketh men merry and preserveth youth. It putteth away fracins, ring worms and all spots of the face, etc. It is mervelous profitable for frantic men and such as be melancoly. It expelleth poison. The smell thereof burnt, killeth flies and cold creeping beasts. It restoreth wine that is turned or putrefied.

It is most wholesome for the stomake, the harte and the liver; it nourisheth blood; it agreeth merveylously and most with men's nature . . . it taketh away sadness, pensiveness; it maketh men merri, witti and encreaseth audacitie.

Already it is plain that experience was being gained in methods of distilling purer spirit. It is probable that the original wine did not contain a very high alcoholic content, thus double distillation would not produce a very strong spirit. Furthermore it would almost certainly have been heavily tainted with fusel oil and similar poisons. A third distillation would produce a much stronger alcohol and a fourth stronger still.

The modern method of distilling malt whisky requires two pot stills, the first of which receives the 'wash' after the malting and brewing processes. The wash is kept at the boil and the vapour is led off through the cooling coil, condensing into what is termed 'low wines'. At this stage it is quite undrinkable. It is then distilled in the second pot still. The first 'run' of liquor, known as the foreshots, containing the higher alcohols, fusel oil and other poisonous impurities, has to be drawn off before the main run, or middle cut, of pure malt whisky is taken off. Finally the aftershots, or feints, the lower alcohols, which again contain impurities and poisonous oils, are also drawn off at the end of the process. Both foreshots and feints are later re-distilled.

The modern pot still is made of copper and is a large enclosed vessel of much the same shape as those depicted as used by the alchemists in the past, with a long narrow neck leading off to the copper coil immersed in cold running water to aid condensation. The still may contain anything from 2,000 gallons upwards. The efficiency of the coil and of the entire process is of course beyond comparison with the 16th century, although the basic principle remains little changed.

The 16th-century stills probably contained anything from four or five gallons to thirty or forty at the very most and without means to assess the quality of the product it must have been a very rough and ready business. Yet even if the coil and methods of condensation were primitive in the extreme, repeated distillation was bound to produce a strong spirit. Unless sufficient experience had been gained to select only the pure spirit and discard the foreshots and feints, however, it would have been extremely dangerous to drink. The assumption must be that the majority of those who knew sufficient about the process had also by this time, learned the art by experience, even if only by tasting the hot spirit as it came from the still and noting the differences.

By 1555 distilling seems to have been common enough in Scotland, for the Scottish Parliament, when passing an Act forbidding the export of victuals in time of famine, expressly excluded 'aqua vite' amongst other goods. As this exemption also applied specifically to Scots living on the west coast and trading with the Western Isles, it is an indication that by this time there was a considerable trade in whisky. Since at about the same time the Bailies of Edinburgh ordered a certain Besse Campbell to cease distilling aqua vitae within the burgh without the barber surgeons' permission, it is plain that distilling was common throughout Scotland.

In 1561, on the death of her husband the Dauphin of France, Mary returned to Scotland to take the crown at the age of 19. After her marriage to Darnley and the birth of a son, destined to be James VI of Scotland, her conduct with Bothwell resulted in her being forced to abdicate in her son's favour in 1567. In 1568 she fled to England for refuge and was imprisoned by Elizabeth for nineteen weary years before her execution. With the 'Virgin Queen' on the English throne the course was set for the Union of the Crowns.

As far as distilling was concerned, the next event of note was the publication in 1578 of Raphael Holinshed's *Chronicles of England, Scotland and Ireland*. These contained references to the various forms of aqua vitae to be found in

9

Scotland which were termed simplex, or twice distilled, composita, thrice distilled, and perfectissima, four times distilled. Also included was a discourse on their medicinal qualities which exceeded that of Peter Morwyng:

Beying moderatelie taken, it sloweth age; it strengtheneth youthe; it helpeth digestion; it cutteth fleume; it abandoneth melancholie; it relisheth the harte; it lighteneth the mynde; it quickeneth the spirites; it cureth the hydropsis; it healeth the strangury; it pounceth the stone; it repelleth grauel; it puffeth awaie ventositie; it kepyth and preserveth the head from whyrling – the eyes from dazelyng – the tongue from lispyng – the mouth from snafflyng – the teethe from chatteryng – the throte from ratlyng – the weasan from stieflyng – the stomach from wamblyng – the harte from swellyng – the bellie from wirthchyng – the guts from rumblyng – the hands from shiueryng – the sinowes from shrinkyng – the veynes from crumplyng – the bones from soakyng . . . trulie it is a soueraigne liquor.

In 1579 there was the first Act in Scotland specifically related to aqua vitae. It is obvious that by this time there had been a very considerable increase in the number of people distilling and from Holinshed it is also clear that the Tudor Englishman had considerable regard for Scots aqua vitae, even if he was already beginning to make his own English 'brandy'. This Act 'anent the making of aquavitie' indicates the effect this increase was having for it prohibited the brewing and distilling of 'aquavitie' from the 1st of December 1579 until the 1st of October 1580, i.e. the customary date for the start of the harvest. Despite this widespread prohibition an exception was made in the case of noblemen, barons and gentlemen brewing and distilling their own malt for their own use.

It must be assumed that there had been a very poor harvest in 1579 and these measures were taken simply to avoid famine, for they were not repeated. It may, however, be that they were found to be ineffective and useless, hence not worth repeating. It is certainly doubtful if they were very strictly observed for clearly they would have been hard to enforce. In a nation where distilling was obviously quite a widespread and common practice and without effective methods of surveillance or enforcement such an Act was not likely to be observed.

Yet, although distilling by this time had become common in England, it was almost entirely the distillation of wine to produce brandy, and it does not seem to have been as prevalent as in Scotland, where it was principally the distillation of malt wash. The Elizabethan Englishman's chief drink was ale. The average house incorporated a brewery and a distillery amongst the outhouses close to the kitchen. The same was undoubtedly the case in Scotland, although most of the architecture of the period was built for defence against attack from England, or in case of civil strife. Such rooms therefore are less easy to locate and may also have had other uses assigned to them.

Despite the onslaught of the Spanish Armada, which in 1588 was scattered and wrecked around the coasts of Britain, Elizabeth's long reign continued unshaken. Meanwhile James VI had carefully bided his time, resisting the efforts of Philip of Spain to win him as an ally. With his cousin's death in 1603, he became James I of England and VI of Scotland. The Union of the Crowns ensured that willy nilly the Scots and the English were allied at last.

2. Union of the Crowns to the Revolution

O Muse! be kind and dinna fash us
To flee awa beyont Parnassus,
Nor seek for Helicon to wash us,
That Heath'nish spring!
Wi' Highland whisky scour our hawses* [*clear our throats]
And gar us sing.

ROBERT FERGUSSON 1750–1774

The Union of the Crowns in the person of James I of England and James VI of Scotland brought peace to the two kingdoms at last and unity in theory, if not entirely in practice. The reivers no longer raided over the borders and a Scottish king, who knew Scotland far better than he ever knew England, ruled in Westminster, but that was about as far as it went. The English were prepared to welcome James as a peaceful solution to the succession which had been causing concern for much of the latter part of Elizabeth's long reign, but the Scots at the royal court in the south were regarded as proud and penurious interlopers.

Despite their Scottish king the English retained a deep suspicion and distrust of the Scots themselves which was fully reciprocated. The Scottish and English Parliaments remained separate bodies with little contact between them. The

12

law and its administration on each side of the border was quite different and destined to remain so. The English Church and the Scots Kirk with its Presbyterian creed had little in common. Trade continued much as before without any great economic benefits to either nation since the English merchants viewed their Scots counterparts as a source of unwanted competition, especially in the growing Colonies overseas, which added resentment on both sides to the underlying mutual distrust and suspicion. Such anti-Scottish sentiments no doubt extended to everything Scots as well, including Scottish aqua vitae.

In the first quarter of the seventeenth century the term aqua vitae began to be used less in England. Such variations as 'brandewine', or more commonly 'brandy wine', were used with increasing frequency instead, denoting a spirit distilled either from wine, or the lees of wine. It is an interesting instance of word survival that the common trade name for industrial alcohol even today is 'trade brandy'.

During the same period the Gaelic term 'uisge beatha' meaning water of life, the equivalent of aqua vitae or eau de vie, began to be used in the Highlands of Scotland. The term 'usquebaugh' was also used alternatively, although originating in Ireland and more common initially there. This denoted a spirit distilled from barley, the forerunner of the whisky we know today. Prior to the use of 'uisge beatha' or 'usquebaugh' there was no clear distinction in Scotland between aqua vitae distilled from barley and that distilled from wine, although clearly, referring back to Friar John Cor, the term covered both as early as 1494.

In his *Itineraries* written between 1605 and 1617, covering England, Scotland and the Continent, Fynes Moryson did not mention spirit drinking amongst the Scots at all, perhaps because his visit north of the border was obviously brief. In a short passage on Scots drinking habits he merely indicated that extremely strong ale was the principal drink and that there were few inns. He wrote:

I did never see nor heare that they have any publike Innes with signes hanging out, but the better sort of Citizens brew Ale their usuall drinke (which will distemper a stranger's bodie) and the same Citizens will entertaine passengers upon acquaintance or entreaty.

Despite the paucity of inns, John Taylor, the eccentric English self-styled water-poet, during his *Pennyless Pilgrimage* in 1618 described the hospitality he received during a visit to Scotland as very nearly overwhelming him at times. Of a visit to Edinburgh he wrote:

13

The worst was that wine and ale was so scarce and the people there such misers of it that every night before I went to bed, if any man had asked me a civil question all the wit in my head could not have given him a sober answer.

On a visit to the Earl of Mar at Braemar in the Highlands he was taken hunting deer in the Highland fashion. Entering into the spirit of the occasion he wore Highland dress and enjoyed himself hugely. He mentioned drinking aqua vitae there, but surprisingly it did not receive a mention elsewhere. The conclusion may be drawn that he simply preferred ale and wine to spirits, which were at that time still not greatly drunk in England. The fact that he drank aqua vitae in the Highlands may also be taken to indicate that it was already being drunk increasingly there as ideally suited to the surroundings and the way of life.

In the same year, 1618, there is the first mention of 'uisge' being drunk at a Highland chieftain's funeral; yet another indication, if it were required, that it was becoming a favourite drink in the Highlands. The shortening and corruption of the Gaelic 'uisge beatha' to 'uisge' and hence to 'whisky' is a natural verbal contraction. Henceforth the term aqua vitae can at last be firmly identified as the whisky it was in due course to become, the water of life of Scotland, no longer to be confused with brandy, the aqua vitae of the Continent distilled from wine. Crude though it may have been, often mixed with cinnamon and herbs, or sometimes with honey and oatmeal, to make it palatable, the modern whisky was slowly developing. Where the malt was dried with peat smoke, this and the pure mountain water must have already been adding its own unique flavour to Highland 'uisge', primitive though it may have been.

By this time, however, at the turn of the 16th century a very clear division was becoming noticeable between Highlands and Lowlands. From the 14th to the middle of the 16th centuries it had not been so obvious, for the Scottish nobles were as treacherous and self-seeking as any in Europe and the Lowland poor, the bulk of the nation, were accustomed to a life of wretchedness and poverty, inured to invasion and insecurity, often on the verge of starvation. In their trackless mountain regions the Highlanders under the clan system, though also often on the verge of starvation, were in many ways more secure. They regularly levied a system of 'black meal' or protection money from their Lowland neighbours in return for ensuring the safety of their cattle, and as a useful warrior reserve in time of war or invasion such behaviour was generally tolerated.

During the Reformation in the latter part of the 16th century many of the Scottish nobility enriched themselves by acquiring church lands and thus welcomed the new faith. The Lowlanders, accustomed to poverty and wretchedness, welcomed the strong, if sometimes harsh, Presbyterian creed with its promise of salvation for true believers. By the turn of the century the bulk of the nation was Presbyterian with the exception of large parts of the inaccessible, mountainous Highlands where the Reformation had scarcely penetrated, simply due to lack of proselytisers.

Whereas the Reformation gave the Lowlanders a much needed spiritual security and the Union of 1603 provided them with security from invasion, the Highlanders and Islanders of the Hebrides remained largely unaffected by either. Still a near pagan, warrior society devoted to the ties of blood kinship of the clan system, the chieftains' prowess in battle and drinking were eulogised in Gaelic verse by the bards of the clan, themselves venerated for their poetic and musical skills. While the Highlanders continued to levy 'black meal' from their Lowland neighbours, the Islanders levied toll in cash or kind from any unarmed boats passing through their waters in return for safe passage. Each continued to indulge in clan feuds, often with considerable loss of life. As late as 1602 the Colquhouns were almost massacred in Dunbartonshire by the Mac-Gregors and so notorious was the latter clan that James decreed its name should be proscribed and no-one henceforth allowed to bear it.

It is apparent that in part at least the poverty and lawlessness of the Highlanders and Islanders was ascribed in the south to overmuch drinking of aqua vitae and wine. In 1609 the chieftains of the Western Isles agreed to certain Statutes of Icolmkill (or Iona), which were drawn up in Edinburgh with a view to improving the situation there on the grounds that:

. . . one of the special causes of the great poverty of the Isles, and of the great cruelty and inhuman barbarity which has been practiced by sundry of the inhabitants upon their natural friends and neighbours, has been their extraordinary drinking of strong wines and aqua vitae brought in among them, partly by merchants of the mainland and partly by traffickers among themselves.

Under these Statutes the Islanders were prohibited from importing wine or aqua vitae, but they were allowed to distil aqua vitae or brew ale for themselves. Barons and gentlemen were permitted to send for wine to the Lowlands for their own use. Any merchant so unwise as to attempt to import any wine for sale was liable to have his entire cargo seized.

15

The sixth Statute dealt with the subject of Education, attributing the 'continuance of barbarity, impiety and incivility' in the Isles to lack of knowledge of English and decreeing that every gentleman must send his eldest son or, if without male issue, his eldest daughter to school in the Lowlands. The object was stated as being that they might learn 'to speik, reid and write Inglische'. The longer-term intention of the Statute, however, was revealed as being that the 'Irishe language which is one of the chief and principall causis of the continewance of barbaritie and incivilitie amongis the inhabitants of the Isles and Heylandis may be abolisheit and removeit'.

As early as 1609 King James VI of Scotland, by this time for six years King James I of England, was engaging along with his Lowland advisers in nothing less than a long-term plan aimed at the extinction of the Gaelic language in both Highlands and Islands. Perhaps not altogether surprisingly, however, these Statutes proved ineffectual and difficult to implement. In 1616 the Privy Council was forced to pass an 'Act agens the drinking of Wynes in the Yllis'.

This Act imposed a penalty of £20 on anyone buying or drinking wine, and the exact amount of wine allowed to the various chieftains was strictly defined. Thus, MacLeod of Dunvegan, MacLean of Duart and MacDonald of Sleat were allowed four tuns of wine a year, amounting to a thousand gallons apiece. Lesser chieftains such as Clanranald were allowed three tuns and, still lower down the scale, Mackinnon of Strath was allowed one tun.

Even this 1616 Act proved ineffectual and in 1622 it had to be re-enacted due to consistent breaking of the peace by unruly chieftains. Nothing it seemed could stop the Islanders' galleys from boarding passing ships to the sad loss of their wine. As late as 1636 Clanranald boarded a ship from England, the *Susannah*, which was laden with wine and slightly off course. As a sop to legality he insisted on the captain 'selling' him the ship as salvage, himself naming the price of £8. Understandably the authorities in the south found it difficult and tiresome to control such activities. Friction between the Gaels in the north and the government in the south and mutual distrust between Highlander and Lowlander increased rather than lessened as the century advanced.

Meanwhile in England the demand for aqua vitae seems to have been steadily increasing by degrees. It seems largely to have been distilled from wine, as a form of brandy, rather than from grain. Yet, though the demand for Scots whisky does not appear to have been great, it does not seem to have been entirely unappreciated. In a letter from Marie Montgomerie to Mr. Secretary Dorchester, dated 5th February 1631, she disclosed that she was sending him 'three little barrels of Scotch accoutie'.

In the year 1636 Charles I granted the Worshipful Company of Distillers their first charter. The Regulations were framed by Sir Theodore de Mayerne, the King's Physician, and the Queen's Physician, Dr. Thomas Cademan, who was made the first Master of the Company. The Regulations stated in part:

No Afterworts, or Wash (of brewers) called Blew John, nor musty, unsavoury or un-wholesome tills, or dregs of beer or ale; nor unwholesome or adulterated wines, or Lees of wines; nor unwholesome sugar-water, musty, unsavoury, or unwholesome returned Beer or Ale; nor rotten, unsavoury or corrupt fruits, druggs, spices, herbs, seeds; nor any other ill-conditioned materials of what kind soever, shall henceforth be distilled, ex-tracted, or drawn into small spirits, or Low Wines, or be in any other way used, directly or indirectly, by any of the Members of this Company, or their successors at any time hereafter for ever.

From the list of prohibited materials it is possible to gauge fairly accurately the sort of ingredients which had gone towards the making of aqua vitae or 'brandy' in England hitherto. By the all-embracing nature of the list it seems that anything available was likely to be pressed into use with small consideration for the end product. Small wonder that the comparatively primitive forms of usquebaugh available were greatly preferred by those Englishmen who knew of them. Although distilling in Scotland was a private matter rather than an industry, obviously the Scots had greater experience and were producing a purer form than the spirits distilled in England.

There was, however, already a cloud on the horizon. Prior to the Civil War in 1642 Charles I had been seeking ways of increasing his income as his expenditure outran his revenue. The Earl of Bedford had been given the task of setting up the first Excise duties. This was, indeed, one of the issues complained of by the Parliamentarians in the 'Grand Remonstrance' of 1641, when it was characterised as 'an unjust and pernicious attempt to extort great payments from the subject by way of excise'. In fact Charles never had the opportunity to impose such an Excise tax before the outbreak of the Civil War. In June of 1641, however, Parliament passed 'A Tonnage and Poundage Act'. This decreed a tax on:

. . . every tun of wine that is or shall come into this realm or any of His Majesty's dominions by way of merchandise the sum of three shillings, and so after that rate, and of every tun of sweet wines as well malmesy as other, that is or shall come into the realm by any merchant alien three shillings, and so after the rate over and above the three shillings above mentioned, and of every awme of Rhenish wine that is or shall come in twelve pence. . . .

Parliament then decided to impose an Excise duty itself but, on the immediate outcry that arose against it, hastily withdrew. Instead they issued a political denial, worthless even then, which, quoted from the Commons Journal of October 1642, reads:

Aspersions were cast by malignant persons upon the house of commons that they intended to introduce excises, the house for its vindication therein did declare, that these rumours were false and scandalous, and that their authors should be apprehended and brought to condign punishment.

The subsequent progress of Excise duty is to be found in Blackstone's *Commentaries*, where he gives the origins of the Excise tax as follows:

Its original establishment was in 1642 and its progress was gradual, being at first laid upon those persons and commodities where it was supposed the hardship would be least perceivable, viz, the makers and vendors of beer, ale, cyder and perry, and the royalists at Oxford soon followed the example of their brethren in Westminster by imposing a similar duty; both sides protesting that it would be continued no longer than to the end of the war, and then be utterly abolished. But the Parliament at Westminster soon after imposed it on flesh, wine, tobacco, sugar and such a multitude of other commodities that it might fairly be denominated general; . . . afterwards, when the nation had been accustomed to it for a series of years . . . openly declared, 'the impost of excise to be the most easy and indifferent levy that could be laid upon the people:' and accordingly continued it during the whole usurpation.

In 1643 the English Parliament imposed Excise duty of 2d on 'every Gallon of Strong Water or Aqua Vitae'. It further decreed a duty of 8d on 'every Gallon of Strong Water perfectly made imported from beyond the Seas'. The phrase 'perfectly made' merely implied fit for consumption, but no distinction was made between twice distilled or four times distilled spirit. It was simply a tax on volume. Furthermore in England the Scots usquebaugh was regarded as 'imported' and therefore subject to the 8d tax, thus imposing a penal tariff on the Scots.

The following year, 1644, the Scots Parliament, allied to the English Parliament by the Solemn League and Covenant, and in urgent need of revenue for its armed forces, followed the English example and went one better. It imposed a duty of 2s 8d 'on everie pynt of aquavytie or strong watteris sold within the country'. Admittedly, since Scots and English measures differed greatly, a Scots pint amounted to nearly a third of a gallon by English standards, but even so such a swingeing tax led to immediate large-scale evasion and proved virtually unenforceable in practice.

During his journeying in Scotland John Taylor had observed the difference between Scottish and English measures. He recorded:

The Scots do allow almost as large a measure for their miles as they do of their drink, for an English gallon, either of ale or wine, is but their quart and one Scottish mile now and then may well stand for a mile and a half or two English.

The actual table of measures in use in Scotland at this time and as late as the end of the 18th century, despite being officially brought into line with the English measures after the Union in 1707, was: four gills equal one mutchkin, two mutchkins equal one chopin and two chopins equal one pint. Compared with English measures, one Scots gill equalled four-fifths of an English gill, one mutchkin equalled three gills, one chopin equalled one pint and two gills, one Scots pint (also known as a 'tappit hen') equalled three English pints and one gallon Scots equalled three gallons English.

The Scottish issues in the Civil War were principally religious. The Scottish National Covenant, signed in an emotional upsurge of feeling in 1638, demonstrated the strength of Presbyterianism in Scotland and the dislike of the Episcopalian innovations proposed by Charles I. The so-called Bishops' Wars of 1639 and 1640, which followed, were theoretically ended by Charles's signature in 1641 agreeing to all the Covenanters' demands. In 1643, however, the Scots allied themselves with the Parliamentary forces against the King in the vain belief that, as the English had agreed to the Solemn League and Covenant, they would attempt to spread Presbyterianism in England.

It was then, despite the fact that he had fought with the Covenanters in the Bishops' Wars, that Montrose placed his sword at Charles's service. As Captain General in 1644 Montrose raised a small force of Highlanders and for a whole year waged a brilliant campaign throughout Scotland. Before being surprised and defeated by Leslie at Philiphaugh outside Selkirk in the Borders in 1645, his Highlanders had driven all before them. By the very success of his generalship Montrose helped to sow even greater fear and distrust of the Highlanders in the Lowland and southern minds.

In 1648 came the second Civil War between Cromwell's forces and Parliament. The following year saw Charles I's execution and the proclamation of Charles II as his successor by the Scots. Charles first sent Montrose on an ill-planned and foredoomed expedition to raise the Highlands once more, which merely resulted in his capture and execution. Then Charles accepted the Covenants and joined the Covenanting forces led by Leslie. In 1650 Cromwell would have been tactically defeated had the Scots retained the advantage of the high ground outside Dunbar. The bigotted ministers of the Kirk overruled Leslie and forced him to attack against his better judgement. The Scots were soundly defeated and within a year the Commonwealth forces were in complete control of the country. When Cromwell was made Protector in 1653 his dictatorship was absolute.

As far as Scotland was concerned the Protector's rule proved unexpectedly enlightened. The barriers on trade between England and Scotland were lifted and free trade encouraged. In 1655 the Excise duty of 2s 8d per Scots pint of 'aquavytie or strong watteris' was drastically reduced to 2s per quart. The year 1657, however, saw the appearance in England of the first 'Excise Gaugers', the Excise officers who possessed powers to gauge, or measure, the vessels used in the distilling process, or in the manufacture or sale of drink. As yet they were restricted to England.

An interesting mention of distilling in Scotland during the interregnum of the Commonwealth occurred in 1655 and was noted in the Session Record of St. Ninian's Church near Stirling. One Robert Hage, tenant of Throsk farm in that parish was accused of distilling on the Sabbath, a considerable misdemeanour in those times of strict religious observance of the Lord's Day. Anyone proven guilty of such an offence was then likely to receive stern punishment. The record in this instance reads:

Compeared Robert Hage being summoned for Sabbath breaking and Wm. Reid, John Groby, William Harley and Christian Eason, Witnesses. Robert Hage denied he knew any such thing as was laid to his charge. The witnesses deponed unanimously that they saw the cauldron on the fyre, and a stand reiking and that they heard the guidwife say, 'the lasse has put on the caldron and played some afterwort' and she knew not whether her cauldron was befor on the fyre on a Sabbath day and had she been at home it should not have been done (for she was byt presentlie cam'd from Alloway Church) So it being only some pynts of small drink played by a servant lasse naither maister nor mistress accessarie to it, upon engagement of Christian carriage for the future, rebuked before the Session.

A hot Still.

A, *Sheweth the bot-tome which ought to be of Copper.*

B, *The Head.*

C, *The barrel filled with cold water to refrigerate and condensate the water and oyl that run through the pipe or worm that is put through it.*

D, *A pipe of brass or pewter, or rather a worm of Tin running through the barrel.*

E, *The Alembick set in the furnace with the fire under it.*

How to make Aqua vitæ *out of Beer.*

Ake of stale strong beer, or rather, the grounds thereof, put it into a copper Still with a worm, distil it gently (or otherwise it will make the head of the Still fly up) and there will come forth a weak Spirit, which is called, low Wine : of which, when thou hast a good quantity, thou maist distil it again of it self, and there will come forth a good *Aqua vitæ.* And if thou distillest it two or three times more, thou shalt have as strong a Spirit as out of Wine ; and indeed, betwixt which, and the Spirit of Wine, thou shalt perceive none or very little difference.

How

Instructions for making aqua vitae, from John French's The Art of Distillation *(1664)*

There are certain points arising from this parish record which are worth considering. 'Some pynts' in Scottish measures could well have amounted to three or more gallons in English measures, even though this was clearly regarded as a very minor matter. The reasonable assumption is therefore that the still had a considerable capacity amounting to a number of gallons. The term 'afterwort' indicates plainly that it was whisky which was being distilled and to judge by the potential size of the apparatus this would appear to have been a commercial rather than a purely private venture. Already it would seem that distilling was regarded as a profitable subsidiary farming enterprise.

Although it may not have been obvious at the time, two actions of the Commonwealth regime were to have a considerable effect on different aspects of drinking in Britain over the ensuing centuries. The immediate result of the introduction of the Excise tax on wines and spirits was widespread evasion and smuggling. The term smuggling came to be recognised as covering both illicit distilling and evasion of tax, also the illicit import of wines or spirits without paying duty. Everyone took it as a matter of course that the tax should be evaded if possible and smuggling was considered perfectly honourable and respectable by all classes of society. This attitude of mind was to persist well into the 19th century. The steadily expanding port-wine trade of the 18th and 19th centuries resulted directly from the Commercial Treaty with Portugal signed in 1654.

On Cromwell's death in 1658 there was a brief hiatus before the Restoration of Charles II in 1660. Those who had confidently looked forward to the repeal of the hated Excise duties were to be sadly disappointed. The introduction of the Gaugers in 1657 was in itself enough to ensure their retention. Admittedly the direct tax on whisky in Scotland was greatly reduced in 1660, varying from 2d to 4d per gallon according to the basic constituents used. In 1661 it was replaced by a tax on malt which was only imposed when a burgh or shire failed to achieve payment of a fixed annual levy.

As far as Scotland was concerned the Restoration meant an end to free trade and a resumption of the old protective tariff barriers. The suspicion, distrust and resentment of the English merchants were now reinforced by a distinct uneasiness at the commercial acumen of their Scots counterparts. Nor was the renewal of anti-Scottish feeling reserved solely to the merchant class. Charles had not forgotten his treatment at the hands of the Scots Covenanters and his contempt for them was dutifully mirrored in varying degrees throughout England.

1, 2   Two 17th-century stills

3   Distilling in the 16th century

A *The Still*	L *A Pewter Crane*
B *The Worm tub*	M *A Pewter Valencia*
C *The Pump*	N *Hippocrates bag or Flannel*
D *Water tub*	*Sleeve*
E *A Press*	O *Poker Fire-shovel Cole rake*
FFF *Tubs to hold the goods*	P *A Box of Bungs*
GGGG *Canns of different size*	Q *The Worm within the Worm tub*
H *A Wood Funnel with a iron nosel*	*markd with prick'd lines*
I *A large Vessel to put the Faint*	R *A Piece of Wood to keep down*
or after runnings	*the Head of the Still to*
K *Tin pump*	*prevent flying of*

P. Fourdrinier Delin et Sculp

4   A distillery in 1729

5 Roderick McDonald's inn, Ross-shire, at the time of
Dr. Johnson's tour of the Highlands

6 Poosie Nancy's inn, Mauchline, in the 18th century

7 *The Secret Still* (early 19th century)

8 Jacobite glass (18th century) for drinking to
'the King over the water'

I wadna gie my ain pint stoup foo a the Quins in vogue

9 'I wadna gie my ain pint stoup . . .' Drawing by David Allan (1744–1796)

10 *A Scotch Wedding* (c. 1811) by William Home Lizars (1788–1859)

11   'And aye we'll taste the barley bree' (Robert Burns, *O, Willie Brew'd a Peck o' Maut*)

12   'Nae mercy, then, for airn or steel' (Robert Burns, *Scotch Drink*)

13 'We'll tak' a cup o' kindness yet' (Robert Burns, *Auld Lang Syne*)

Although the Restoration was a period of heavy drinking throughout England, an extract from a *Modern Account of Scotland* (1670) indicates that even in this respect the Scots could do nothing right in English eyes:

The nobility show themselves very great before strangers. They are conducted into the house by many of their servants, where the Lord with his troop of shadows receives them with the grand paw; then enter into some discourse of their country, till you are presented with a great queigh of syrup of bees; after that a glass of white wine, then a rummer of claret, and sometimes after that a glass of sherry-sack; and then begin the round with ale again, and ply you briskly for it is their way of showing you are welcome, to make you drunk.

An indication of the state of affairs in England about the same period is obtained from a petition presented to Parliament in 1673 aimed at prohibiting the import of brandy, rum, coffee and tea. An extract reads:

Before Brandy, which has now become common and is sold in every little alehouse, came to England in such quantities as it now doth, we drank good strong beer and ale, and all laborious people (which are far the greater part of the kingdom) and their bodies requiring after hard labour some strong drink to refresh them did therefor every morning and evening used to drink a pot of ale or a flagon of strong beer, which greatly helped the promotion of our own grains and did them no great prejudice; it hindereth not their work, nor did it take away their senses, nor cost them much money. . . .

Already the strong upsurge in spirit drinking which took place in England during the first half of the 18th century was foreshadowed, although as yet the consumption was not very great, at least by comparison with what was to come in the sordid 'Gin Era' between 1725 and 1750. As yet the Distillers Company exercised a degree of control over the standards of spirits distilled, despite the fact that some distillers blatantly claimed they were conferring a favour on the public by utilising inferior grain unfit for human consumption. The general standard of spirit produced was certainly not as high as that in Scotland. In 1678 Sir Robert Murray wrote of Scottish malting as follows:

Malt is there made of no other grain but barley, whereof there are two kinds, one which hath four rows of grain in the ear, the other two rows. The first is more commonly used, but the other makes the best malt.

Bere is the most ancient form of barley with four rows of spikelets, traces of which have been found in excavations dating back to prehistoric times, but for all that it is said to give a greater spirit yield. Although the other form of barley was more favoured for making malt for ale, bere was probably preferred by many for malt for whisky distilling. At this time the Scots seem to have been very thorough in supervising standards of both ale and whisky and the magistrates appointed officials to check on the standards supplied by the taverns, which were now becoming common in the Lowlands, although still unknown in the Highlands where the laws of hospitality were such that no stranger could be turned away. As yet ale remained the drink of the mass of the Scots and claret was still favoured by the upper classes. Whisky continued to be drunk more in the Highlands than elsewhere.

James II, who succeeded Charles in 1685, suffered all the failings of the Stuarts with none of their redeeming charm or ability. Within three years his obvious leanings towards Roman Catholicism and his fatal Stuart knack of making the wrong decisions had alienated almost all his erstwhile supporters. Most of those who had welcomed the Restoration as willingly welcomed the Revolution when Parliament offered the Crown to James's son-in-law Prince William of Orange in 1688. James, wavering and faint-hearted, fled for the Continent without any real attempt at resistance as he saw his support dwindling before his eyes. William III and Mary succeeded him as King and Queen virtually unopposed in England.

The only real resistance William's supporters, the Whigs, encountered was in Scotland, where John Graham of Claverhouse, Viscount Dundee, raised a Highland army against William in 1689 only a month after he had been crowned. In an attempt to follow Montrose's example, Claverhouse succeeded in defeating a government force at Killiecrankie though mortally wounded in the process. James's choice as his successor, Colonel Alexander Cannon of Galloway, was cordially disliked by the Highlanders and when, soon afterwards, they were defeated at Dunkeld they dispersed in disgust at his poor leadership.

Despite the defeat at Dunkeld the Highlands remained in a turbulent and troubled state. When James, with his fatal ability to compound an error, sent Colonel Cannon back to the Highlands in 1690 it says much for the Highlanders' loyalty to the Stuart cause that they raised an army to follow him again. They were surprised at dawn by a government force while encamped in the Haughs of Cromdale and dispersed with little loss on either side. For the moment this put an end to James's hopes of a Highland rising, but the obvious unrest alarmed William and his advisers in the south. Later in 1690 Fort William was built at the head of Loch Linnhe to exercise a measure of control in the west and help to keep the peace among the clans.

Amongst William III's more zealous supporters in Scotland was the Whig lawyer and politician, Duncan Forbes of Culloden. In 1688 and 1689 he played a prominent part in the anti-Jacobite movement and during his absence in 1689 a force of about 700 'Highland rebels', or Royalists, depending on the viewpoint, sacked his estates near Inverness. Among other damage they burned down his 'ancient brewary of aquavity in Cromarty' for which he promptly put in a claim for compensation amounting to around £4,500. In lieu of this the Scots Parliament granted him and his descendants the right to distil whisky from grain grown on their own land duty free. The Act passed in 1690 is of interest as being the first mention of an individual distillery; it reads:

At Edinburgh, 22nd July, 1690

Our Sovereign Lord and Ladye, the King and Queen's Majesties and the three Estates of Parliament: Considering that the lands at Ferintosh were an ancient Brewary of Aquavity; and were still in use to pay a considerable Excise to the Treasury, while of late they were laid waste of the King's enemies; and it being just to give such as have suffered all possible encouragement, and also necessary to use all lawful endeavours for upholding of the King's Revenue; Therefore their Majesties and the Estates of Parliament for encouragement to the possessors of the said Lands to set up again and prosecute their former trade of brewing and pay a duty of Excyse as formerly; do hereby Ferm for the time to come the yearly Excyse of the said lands of Ferintosh to the present Duncan Forbes of Culloden, and his Successors, Heritors of the same for the sum of 400 merks Scots. . . .

3. Boyle's Hydrometer 1675 to Captain Burt 1726

Sages their solemn een may steek
An' raise a philosophic reek,
An' physically causes seek,
In climes and season:
But tell me whisky's name in Greek,
I'll tell the reason.

The Author's Earnest Cry and Prayer . . .,
ROBERT BURNS 1785/6

In the time of Elizabeth the strength and quality of spirit, or what came to be termed 'proof', was tested by lighting a given amount and measuring the liquid remaining. Another test involved soaking gunpowder in spirit. When ignited, if it exploded, it was over proof; if it burned steadily it was proof, and if it was hard to light it was under proof. In yet another method spirit was poured into a 'proof phial', or glass container, shaken hard and the number of 'beads', or bubbles, then formed were noted. In grain spirit such beads form readily on the surface when the spirit is strong and an estimate of strength could thus be made. These and other rough and ready methods of estimating 'proof' were tried in turn, but were subject to considerable variation. 'Proof' as such, though indicating a spirit of tested strength and quality, could not be accurately defined until an exact method of testing was devised and introduced in the early 19th century.

It was not until after the Restoration, in 1675, that Robert Boyle, noted scientist and inventor, re-discovered the principle of the hydrometer, originally attributed to Archimedes. In the *Philosophical Transactions* of June 1675 Boyle described his hydrometer as the 'New Essay Instrument . . . consisting of a bubble furnished with a long and slender stem, which was to be put into several liquors to compare and estimate their specific gravities'.

With various improvements the instrument, although still by no means accurate for any fine degree of testing, was soon being applied for revenue purposes as a test of whether spirit was over or under 'proof'. Thus in 1688 the first Act was introduced in England laying down a duty on 'every gallon of single brandy, spirits or aqua vitae imported from beyond the seas to be paid by the importer before landing, over and above the duties already payable for the same'. A duty of 4s was laid on 'every gallon of brandy spirits, or aqua vitae above proof, commonly called double brandy. . . .' For the first time an attempt was being made to charge duty by strength rather than volume. This was to become increasingly the method of taxation, but as the first Act to differentiate between the strength of various spirits this was a notable piece of legislation.

Upon the outbreak of war with France in 1690 another important Act of Parliament concerning distilling was passed in a misguided effort to provide the English corn growers with protection by giving any Englishman the right to distil spirits from home-grown corn. The Act stated:

An Act for the encouraging of the distillation of Brandy and spirits from corn. First, the trade and commerce of France being prohibited, and all their goods from being imported in this kingdom; And whereas good and wholesome Brandy, *aqua vitae* and spirits may be made and drawn from corn; for the encouragement of the making of brandy, strong waters and spirits from malted corn, and for the greater consumption of corn and the advantage of tillage in this kingdom, the King, Queen and Parliament then assembled have thus ordained it. . . .

Such an Act, the first openly linking distilling with farming, did not discourage the smugglers, or free traders, as they preferred to be called. Even in time of war they continued to evade the payment of Excise duties by smuggling brandy, spirits, wine and silks from France, or even usquebaugh and other goods from Scotland. Despite the attempts of the Distillers Company to retain some control over the standards of distilling, the inevitable effect of the Act was for the standards of spirits produced in England to sink considerably. The way was being paved for the descent to the sordid depths of the 'Gin Era' in the early 18th century.

Meanwhile in Scotland the Highlands remained in a state of unrest, the cause of deep disquiet and distrust in the Lowlands, especially in governmental circles where memories of Montrose's successful campaign of 1645 were still disturbingly vivid. The profound hate, inspired largely by fear and ignorance, which motivated many Lowlanders in their dealings with the Highlanders is hard to understand today. By the end of the 17th century, however, the vast differences between Highlander and Lowlander, by no means so plain in the previous century, were becoming increasingly marked. The Highlanders' great weakness was that they were not united among themselves. The Campbells, who had been led by the politically opportunist Duke of Argyll against Montrose were universally hated by the other clans, but old feuds and fresh quarrels were liable to arise amongst them at any time.

In a *History of the Revolution in Scotland* printed in Edinburgh in 1690 this commonly held opinion of the Highlanders appeared:

The Highlanders of Scotland are the sort of wretches that have no other consideration of honour, friendship, obedience or government, than as, by alteration in affairs or revolution in the government, they can improve to themselves an opportunity of robbing or plundering their neighbours.

All too often the Lowlander regarded the Highlander as an ignorant, half-naked, armed savage, speaking a different language and, worst of all sins in the eyes of a perfervid Presbyterian, a Roman Catholic, virtually a heathen. The Highlander at this stage merely regarded the Lowlander with a certain amused contempt. Neither remotely understood the other. Perhaps their one common meeting ground was a mutual liking for usquebaugh, although the principal drink of the Lowland masses was still ale.

The effect of the notorious massacre of the Macdonalds of Glencoe in 1692 was to turn the tables and imbue the Highlanders with a deep distrust and disquiet regarding the Sassenach (i.e., the Southerners, as the Lowlanders were known to the Gael). The breach of trust and abuse of the sacred Highland code of hospitality sowed an ineradicable distrust in the Highlanders' minds. It was this as much as loyalty to the Stuarts which was among the deep-seated reasons for the rebellions of 1715 and 1745. Since it contributed considerably to the eventual opening up of the Highlands, which in turn ultimately resulted in the development of Scotch whisky on a national scale, it is as well to understand what was involved.

In an effort to pacify the Highlands after the Battle of Cromdale, the chieftains of the various clans were commanded to lodge an oath of submission by January 1st 1692 or be outlawed. Due partly to natural obstinacy and procrastination and partly to a misunderstanding, the elderly chief of the Macdonalds of Glencoe, MacIan, left it too late. He arrived before the Sheriff in Fort William to make his submission in time, only to find that he was supposed to take the oath before the Sheriff in Inveraray. Owing to heavy snowfalls he did not arrive there until the 6th of January. He then took the oath and word was passed that he had done so to the authorities in Edinburgh.

Sir John Dalrymple (the Secretary of State), together with the Master of Stair (the Lord Advocate, later Earl of Stair) and the Earl of Breadalbane (neighbour, but no friend, to the Macdonalds), seem to have connived behind the scenes. When the register reached the Privy Council in Edinburgh the name of Macdonald of Glencoe had been erased. With advisers heavily biased against the Highlanders it is not surprising that William III signed the following order, now amongst the Culloden Papers:

To Coll. Hill 16th Jany 1692.
If M'Ean of Glenco and that trybe can be well separated from the rest, it will be a proper vindication of the public Justice to extirpate that sect of thieves. The double of this instruction is only communicated to Sir Tho. Livingston. W. Rex.

The phrasing is suspiciously close to that in a letter Stair wrote at the time, which ended: 'Let it be secret and sudden'. On his instructions a hundred and twenty Campbell soldiers, old enemies of the Macdonalds, were billeted in the glen, arriving under guise of friendship, led by Campbell of Glenorchy, whose niece was married to MacIan's son. At a chosen hour at night ten days later reinforcements were to arrive from Ballachulish and the other end of the glen was to be blocked by troops from Breadalbane. In all nearly a thousand men were to be mobilised to turn the glen into a death trap for the two hundred and fifty Macdonalds living there, of whom only fifty could be rated as fighting men. The fatal day was to be February 13th.

In the event it was a case of bureaucratic butchery botched. On the chosen day a blizzard was raging. The expected reinforcements failed to arrive. The Campbells' hearts were not in their task, for though hereditary enemies they were not inhuman. Some had given indirect warnings to their hosts, others took care to alert the houses as they approached in darkness to allow the occupants time to escape. Eventually a mere thirty-eight men, women and children were killed in the glen, though probably as many perished in the hills from wounds and exposure. It fell far short of the total 'extirpation' expected, but the cold-blooded planning with intent to murder an entire clan in their beds using troops sent in peace and friendship still makes it stand out as one of the more infamous examples of treachery of all time. William III, who had, wittingly or unwittingly, signed the order, became the most loathed and hated man in the Highlands.

When news of the affair leaked out an enquiry was ordered from London, not from Edinburgh, but needless to say little came of it. In any event the damage had already been done. Like the Plains Indians in the Mid-West of America over a century later, the Highlanders and their clan system were insufficiently equipped to withstand the advances of civilisation. As the Indians had a deep distrust and contempt for the white man so the Highlanders had a deep distrust and contempt for the Lowlanders and the administrators in the south.

The methods first introduced by James I and VI in the 1609 Statutes of Icolmkill (or Iona) attacking the clan system through the medium of the Gaelic language were being vigorously extended by the end of the century. It is only necessary to quote a part of one of the Acts of William III 'for rooting out the Erse language and for other *pious* uses' to make clear the methods being used. The Society for the Propagation of Christian Knowledge, filled with missionary ardour, considered breaking the clan system and curbing the use of the Gaelic language the only means of conversion to their faith. Such crusading zeal is always hard to withstand, even without government backing, and the hard-drinking, supposedly 'heathen' Highlanders and Islanders were a natural target for the earnest Lowland Presbyterians.

Martin Martin, writing about 1695 in his *Description of the Western Isles of Scotland*, indicated that the Islanders had developed their own version of the old simplex, composita and perfectissima. He recorded:

Their plenty of corn was such, as disposed the natives to brew several sorts of liquor, as common usquebaugh, another called trestarig, *id est* aqua-vitae, three times distilled, which is strong and hot: a third sort four times distilled, and this by the natives is called usquebaugh-baul, *id est* usequebaugh, which at first taste affects all the members of the body; two spoonfuls of this last liquor is a sufficient dose; and if any man exceed this, it would presently stop his breath, and endanger his life. The trestarig and usquebaugh-baul are both made of oats.

It would seem that the twice distilled simplex, or usquebaugh, was made from malted barley and was in fact malt whisky, but the stronger spirit was distilled from oats. Making spirit from grain other than barley subsequently appears to have been practised particularly in the Lowlands. In the larger Lowland distilleries of the late 18th century the spirit was indeed often made from grain other than barley and even from roots as well.

Yet, despite the undoubted fact that the Highlanders and Islanders at this time drank great quantities of whisky, or spirits, it is unlikely that they paid much tax on it. The evasion of duty, or smuggling in various forms, was almost a national pastime, both in Scotland and England. In many of the Border towns it was almost the sole occupation, having proved a satisfactory substitute for border raiding. Even so there were few taxes to cause serious complaint in Scotland until the Union of 1707.

In 1681 the malt tax, hitherto only an occasional levy, was made general. Then in 1693 a duty of 2s a pint was imposed on spirits, once again a tax on volume rather than on strength, and in 1695 the malt tax, which had proved unpopular, was dropped. In the time-honoured fashion of the Revenue, however, giving with the one hand and taking with the other, with the removal of the malt tax the duty per pint was increased by a further 3d. All the same, without the Gaugers, the hated Revenue inspectors, already an accepted feature of the English Excise, the Scots had little reason for complaint, at least on the grounds of taxation.

The Scots did, however, have grounds for complaint at the protective tariffs levied on their goods by the English. Furthermore any Scots merchants overseas in America, India, the West Indies, or other colonies, encountered considerable jealousy and opposition from their English opposite numbers, who generally had the ear of the local governor. Despite being treated as aliens, the fact that the Scots tended to support each other clannishly and were often eminently successful, due to their natural business acumen and sheer hard work, merely increased the friction. Those few Scots who moved to London also found it hard to surmount the barriers of prejudice and dislike they encountered.

The situation got worse rather than better. The final years of the 17th century saw the ill-fated attempt by William Paterson, who had made a fortune in the West Indies and assisted in founding the Bank of England, to start a colony at Darien, now Panama. Although originally intended as a joint Scots and English venture, the English merchants concerned grew alarmed at the extent of Scottish participation and persuaded the English Parliament to veto the plan. Thus it was eventually a purely Scottish expedition that set out in 1698 heavily backed by Scottish capital.

Approximately 4,000 Scottish would-be colonists arrived in Darien towards the end of 1698, but from the start everything went wrong. Attacked by the Spanish, who claimed the land, they were refused aid by the English in the West Indies or in North America. Yellow fever and the climate proved even greater opponents than the Spanish. By 1700 it was apparent that the colonists were virtually wiped out and thousands of Scottish investors were ruined. Rightly or wrongly, once again, it was William III who received the blame. Throughout the Lowlands, as well as the Highlands, both he and the English were cursed. Even before the Union of the Crowns such a depth of anti-English feeling had seldom been known.

The Darien disaster was but one of the issues which exacerbated relations between the two nations. The subjects of the succession and free trade were others. While it was agreed that Anne, daughter of James II and VII, should succeed William, the English Parliament passed an Act of Settlement decreeing Sophia, Electress of Hanover, James I and VI's grand-daughter, as next in line, without first consulting the Scots Parliament. The Scots regarded this as an insult and, soon after Anne's succession on William's death in 1702, the Scots countered with their own Act of Security. This laid down that Anne's successor would not be acceptable to them unless he or she agreed to free religion, free government and free trade for Scotland. The English countered by passing the Alien Act threatening a complete trade embargo unless the Scots agreed to their choice.

While tempers waxed hot on both sides and war seemed imminent in 1706, fortunately cooler heads prevailed and the two countries agreed to a meeting of thirty-two chosen Commissioners from each side to work out a Treaty of Union. The proposals put forward by the Commissioners were then put to the two Parliaments for their approval. After lengthy discussion over three months and profound dissension throughout the country, the Scots Parliament finally agreed to the Union of the Parliaments in January 1707.

By this Treaty of Union England and Scotland became one nation called Great Britain. They were to have one flag consisting of the Cross of St. Andrew, the patron saint of Scotland, and the Cross of St. George, the patron saint of England. Taxation was to become uniform and there was to be free trade with similar coinage, weights and measures. The laws and law courts were to remain unchanged. Scotland was to have forty-five members in the House of Commons and sixteen members in the Upper House. The effects on trade and industry in Scotland were ultimately to be very considerable.

Acts of Parliament, however, do not change attitudes of mind overnight. Both England and Scotland suffered from deeply ingrained feelings of dislike and distrust for each other. In many ways the Union was merely to make these feelings more pronounced until time and the mutual benefits apparent on both sides had begun to ease the animosity and depth of feeling. Yet certain attitudes of mind were so deep-rooted that two centuries were to pass before they showed signs of being overcome, and even then they were occasionally still apparent. The treatment of the Scotch whisky industry as late as the twentieth century is a case in point.

In 1708, in an opportunist effort to distract the English during the War of the Spanish Succession, which was being waged throughout most of Anne's reign, the French sent a fleet to the Firth of Forth with James III and VIII, the Old Pretender, and 6,000 troops. Intercepted by the English navy on reaching their destination they lost a warship and several transports and were forced to return to France without landing. This was probably the nearest James ever came to success for it was the widely held opinion at the time that discontent with the Union was so great that, had he landed, he would have carried all before him regardless of the Kirk's distrust for his religion. Despite hazards such as this and mounting economic pressures and discontent during the first decade or so, the Union was to remain firm, for the long-term advantages were soon plain.

Miss Elizabeth Mure, who died in 1795, in her *Observations on the Change in Manners in My Own Times 1700–1790*, noted the effects of the Union as follows:

The change in manners in the new generation was very remarkable. The Union with England carried many of our nobility and gentry to London. Sixty of the most considerable people [i.e. Members of Parliament] being obliged to pass half the year there would no doubt change their Ideas. Besides, many English came to reside at Edinr. The Court of Exchequer and the Bourds of Customs and Excise were mostly all of that nation; at least all the under officers were. These were people of fashion and were well received by the first people here. As the intercourse with the English opened our Eyes a little so it gave us a liberty of Trade we had not had before. From the Union many of our younger Sons became merchants and went abroad. . . .

Early 18th-century woodcut of John Barleycorn, the personification of malt liquor

It is apparent from Miss Mure's *Observations* that the Scots were not slow to take advantage of equal opportunities in overseas trade. Where Scots participation in trade had been minimal during the 17th century there was a great increase during the 18th century. At the same time one of the early effects of the Union was the establishment of Customs and Excise offices staffed mainly by Englishmen. The introduction of Gaugers was far from popular and led to a further increase in evasion and smuggling. Throughout the 18th century, indeed, illegal distilling and smuggling were to become almost recognised occupations in both Scotland and England.

In England, concerned at that time with the war in Europe, one of the first Acts of Anne's reign had been in continuation of William's policy on distilling: 'An Act for encouraging the consumption of malted corn for the better preventing the running of French and Foreign Brandy'. Misguidedly the government went on to withdraw the privileges of the Worshipful Company of Distillers, which at least had provided a measure of control over distilling. Without their supervision, however lax, there was virtually no control over the sort of spirit distilled and the way was now clear for the 'Gin Era' of the following decades.

Another effect of the war with France was that French wine as well as brandy became harder to obtain. The vintners seem to have found their own way round that difficulty for, according to Addison in *The Spectator* in 1709:

There is in this city a certain fraternity of chymical operators who work underground in holes, caverns and dark retirements, to conceal their mysteries from the eyes and observations of mankind. These subterranean philosophers are daily employed in the transmigration of liquors, and by the power of magical drugs and incantations raise under the streets of London the choicest products of the hills and valleys of France. They can squeeze Bordeaux out of a sloe, and Champagne from an apple.

When the Treaty of Utrecht ended the war in Europe in 1713, Parliament attempted to impose a tax on malt in Scotland. At the time of the Union malt had been taxed in England but not Scotland and the Scots exemption had been a major issue prior to final agreement. One of the Articles of the Union, however, contained a qualifying clause, 'during the present war', and the English farmers, resentful at Scots immunity, pressed for their inclusion. The attempt caused an uproar in Scotland where, viewing it as a breach of the Union, the cry of 'Free Malt' was loudly raised. Vetoed later by the House of Lords, the proposal came to nothing and the disturbance in Scotland subsided, though it was a pointer to what was to come.

When Queen Anne died the following year the Jacobite Stuart supporters were without a leader and without plans. The German-speaking George I of Hanover was duly crowned and acclaimed by both English and Scots without opposition. Late as ever, James, the Old Pretender, was only finally proclaimed King in September 1715 when his standard was raised at Braemar by the Earl of Mar. Vain and ambitious, vacillating and indecisive, once a strong supporter of the Union, by this time a bitter opponent, Mar had failed to gain recognition from George I and felt himself slighted. His powers of generalship were small and his grasp of tactics nil, but it is a measure of Highland discontent that, even so, some 6,000 Highlanders joined him at once and the figure later rose to 12,000.

The rebellion was brief and ineffectual. The only opposition consisted of some 2,500 soldiers in Stirling under the Earl of Argyll, but instead of pressing southwards Mar was content to occupy Perth and remain there for nearly two months.

An indecisive action was fought at Sheriffmuir in November and by the time James belatedly arrived in December the rising was all but over By the end of January 1716 the remaining Jacobite forces had withdrawn to Montrose and from there James sailed to France, never to return. The Old Pretender's attempt to secure his throne had proved an utter failure.

Faced with the apparently insoluble problem of perennial unrest in the Highlands, the authorities remained at a loss until the appointment of General George Wade as Commander-in-Chief of the forces in Scotland in 1724. He surveyed the Highlands thoroughly and produced his report and the first sound plan for containing any future uprising. He proposed building Fort Augustus at the foot of Loch Ness and Fort George beyond Inverness in addition to Fort William already built, thus providing a line of forts cutting off the west from the east. He also proposed building two hundred and fifty miles of military roads and over forty bridges to provide easy access for troops between these forts. In conjunction with a Disarming Act, whereby the Highlanders were forbidden to carry arms and were ordered to hand in their weapons, Wade's plan was put into effect in 1725.

Prior to starting work on his roads, which was to take him eleven years, Wade found himself involved in riots in Glasgow, known as the Malt Tax Riots. Ostensibly these were riots among the citizens of Glasgow demonstrating against the attempt to impose a tax of 3d a bushel on malt. In practice they were a general expression of public disgust at what was regarded as a breach of the Union and as such there is little doubt that the Glasgow magistrates connived at them, turning a blind eye to the proceedings.

In 1725 Sir Robert Walpole's government at first proposed a tax of an extra 6d a barrel on ale in Scotland. There was such immediate opposition that this was changed to a tax on malt at 3d a bushel, or half the rate of tax in England. It must have been appreciated how unpopular this tax would be and the estimated revenue was little more than £20,000 so that the assumption must be that it was little more than an assertion of governmental authority.

When the Excise officers tried to collect the tax in Glasgow on the 23rd of June the maltsters refused to let them into their warehouses. A mob soon began to assemble and some fairly serious rioting ensued. On the 24th two companies of infantry under a Captain Bushell marched from Dumbarton in pouring rain. The weather may have had the effect of temporarily damping the spirits of the mob, for when Captain Bushell reported to Provost Miller the latter took the view that the presence of the troops was only likely to inflame the situation.

That evening, however, an M.P., Mr. Daniel Campbell, known to favour the government, had his house burned down. When Provost Miller ordered the troops to make some arrests the next day the mob broke open the gaol and released the prisoners. Soon the soldiers were being heavily stoned and eventually Captain Bushell ordered them to open fire. Matters then got completely out of hand and the mob broke open the town's magazine and armed themselves. By this time thoroughly alarmed, Provost Miller ordered the troops to return to Dumbarton and they had to make a fighting withdrawal, killing about a dozen people in the process.

Since several other towns promptly followed the example set by the Glasgow maltsters, refusing to allow Excise officers into their warehouses, the situation looked serious. It became necessary to make an example of the lawbreakers in Glasgow. Hence General Wade was sent with an impressive force of dragoons and infantry to institute an enquiry. Provost Miller and the town bailies, or magistrates, were examined as to why they had not taken firmer action and as to what they knew of the riots. Their explanations were weak in the extreme and they professed to knowing practically nothing about the entire event.

As a result of the enquiry Provost Miller and three bailies were placed under close arrest and marched off under guard to Edinburgh. After four days in prison they were finally released on bail and received a heroes' welcome from the citizens of Glasgow, of whom they had professed to be terrified, on their return to the city. Ultimately finding any evidence against anyone proved almost impossible as there was a conspiracy of silence on all sides. The Town Council was ordered to pay compensation of £6,080 to Mr. Daniel Campbell for the loss of his house, but despite southern promptings the Provost and bailies were never brought to trial. For his part in the affair Captain Bushell was indicted but received a free pardon. The malt tax remained in being despite its unpopularity.

The effects of the tax during the next half century were to be far-reaching. Ale began slowly to grow less popular, since either the quality suffered, or the price increased, to cover the extra tax. Whisky slowly but steadily began to replace it in popularity as the drink of the people. In licensed distilleries in the Lowlands, in an effort to minimise the effects of the tax, the distillers increasingly began to use unmalted grain with malted barley, thus reducing the quality of the whisky they produced and incidentally encouraging the sales of illicitly distilled whisky made from malted barley which had not paid tax.

Having completed his enquiry in Glasgow, General Wade promptly started on his road-making task in the Highlands in 1726. The new roads, all two hundred and fifty miles of them, were not finished until 1737. They were commemorated in the much repeated and extremely feeble couplet produced by Governor Caulfield of Fort George. As Joseph Mitchell put it in his *Reminiscences*, giving Caulfield rather more than his due: 'Few poets for a single couplet have obtained such immortality'. The couplet runs:

> Had you seen these roads before they were made,
> You'd lift up your hands and bless General Wade.

From the letters of a Captain Edward Burt, who was an engineer officer dealing with Wade's Highland road-making work, we learn a good deal about the Highlands, about the Highlanders and about the drink available there, amongst many other details. Despite a certain obvious bias he was a keen observer with a descriptive pen. When stationed in the Highlands from 1726 onwards he wrote as follows:

We have one great advantage . . . that is, wholesome and agreeable drink, I mean French claret, which is to be met with almost every-where . . . but the concourse of my countrymen has raised the price of it considerably. At my first coming it was but sixteen pence a bottle and now it is raised to two shillings, although there be no more duty paid upon it now than there was before, which, indeed, was often none at all.

French brandy, very good, is about three shillings and sixpence or four shillings a gallon, but in quantities, from hovering ships on the coast, it has been bought for twentypence. . . .

The two-penny as they call it, is their common ale, the price of it is two pence for a Scots pint, which is two quarts. . . . This liquor is disagreeable to those who are not used to it, but time and custom will make almost anything familiar. The malt which is fired with peat . . . gives to the drink a taste of that kind of fuel . . . when the natives drink plentifully of it, they interlace it with brandy or usky. . . .

Regarding whisky he wrote '. . . usky . . . though a strong spirit, is to them like water. And this I have often seen them drink out of a scallop shell'. Perhaps the best comment attributed to him, however, was:

> The glory of the country was usky.

4. Captain Burt in 1727 to Colonel Thornton in 1784

Thee Ferintosh! O sadly lost!
Scotland lament from coast to coast!
Now colic-grips an' barkin hoast,* [*cough]
May kill us a':
For loyal Forbes' charter'd boast
Is ta'en awa!

Scotch Drink, ROBERT BURNS 1786

Captain Burt's letters reveal the staggering amount of whisky which was already being drunk in the Highlands. He noted:

Some of the Highland gentlemen are immoderate drinkers of usky, even three or four quarts at a sitting; and in general the people that can pay the purchase, drink it without moderation. . . . They say for excuse, the country requires a great deal; but I think they mistake a habit and a custom for necessity. . . .

He went on to quote figures:

The collector of the customs at Stornway in the Isle of Lewis told me, that about 120 families drink yearly 4,000 English gallons of this spirit and brandy together, although many of them are so poor they cannot afford to pay for much of either, which you know must increase the quantity drank by the rest; and that they frequently give to children of six or seven years old, as much at a time as an ordinary wine-glass will hold.

He described an occasion when some of his brother officers challenged some Highlanders to a drinking bout in whisky:

Not long ago, four English officers took a fancy to try their strength in this bow of Ulysses against a like number of the country champions; but the enemy came off victorious; and one of the officers was thrown into a fit of gout, without hopes; another had a most dangerous fever; a third lost his skin and hair by the surfeit; and the last confessed to me that when the drunkeness and debate ran high, he took several opportunities to sham it.

Captain Burt concluded that whisky drinking in large quantities was a bad thing. He recorded:

They . . . pretend it does not intoxicate in the Hills as it would do in the Low country, but this . . . I doubt . . . those who drink it to any degree of excess behave, for the most part, like true barbarians, I think much beyond the effect of other liquors. . . .

Of course it is obvious that Captain Burt was primarily a wine drinker and by the standards of the day he was certainly not a heavy drinker. Furthermore he spent the precise years from 1726 and 1727 onwards in Scotland, after George II had succeeded to the throne, when the Gin Era in England was just beginning to become noticeable, or he might not have written quite so smugly. It was about the same time that the comment was made in *The Gentleman's Magazine* that 'one half of the town seems set up to furnish poison to the other half'. The figures speak for themselves. In 1694, with a population of six million, the spirits consumed amounted to about 800,000 gallons a year. By 1730, with a population barely increased by a quarter of a million, the annual consumption had risen to around five million gallons. Yet this was only the beginning. It was to grow much worse before sanity returned.

Beside the scenes which ensued in London when the Gin Era was at its peak Burt's description of 'Bumper' John Forbes of Culloden's manner of entertaining his guests seems positively decorous:

There lives in our neighbourhood, at a house (or castle) called Culloden, a gentleman whose hospitality is almost without bounds. It is a custom of that house, at the first visit or introduction, to take up your freedom by cracking his nut (as he terms it), that is, a cocoa-shell, which holds a pint filled with champagne, or such other sort of wine as you shall choose. . . . Few go away sober at any time; and for the greatest part of his guests, in the conclusion, they cannot go at all.

This he partly brings about by artfully proposing (after the public healths, which always imply bumpers) such private ones as he knows will pique the interest or inclinations of each particular guest of the company whose turn it is to take the lead to begin it in a brimmer; and he himself being always cheerful, and sometimes saying good things, his guests soon lose their guard and then – I need say no more.

For my own part, I stipulated with him, upon the first acquaintance, for the liberty of retiring when I thought convenient; and as such perseverance was made a point of honour, that I might do it without reproach.

As the company are disabled one after another, two servants, who are all the while in waiting take up the invalids with short poles in their chairs, as they sit (if not fallen down) and carry them to their beds; and still the hero holds out.

I remember, one evening an English officer, who has a good deal of humour, feigned himself drunk, and acted his part so naturally, that it was difficult to distinguish it from reality; upon which the servants were preparing to take him up and carry him off. He let them alone until they had fixed the machine, and then raising himself up on his feet, made them a sneering bow, and told them he believed there was no occasion for their assistance; whereupon one of them with *sang froid* and a serious air, said: 'No matter, sir, we shall have you by and by'. This laird keeps a plentiful table, and excellent wines of various sorts and in great quantities; as, indeed he ought, for I have often said I thought there was as much wine spilt in his hall, as would content a moderate family.

Duncan Forbes, Lord President of the Council, was to succeed his brother, 'Bumper' John, as Laird of Culloden. When it is considered just what a valuable grant Lord President Forbes had received in 1690 for the damage to his estate at Ferintosh during the Revolution it is not surprising that any member of the Forbes family should keep open house in this fashion. In return for the annual payment of 400 Scots merks, or £22, he and his descendants were allowed to distil from the grain produced on his 1,800 acre estate without paying any duty. He was not long in taking full advantage of the grant. To replace the one distillery burned down he appears to have built no less than four, which produced more whisky than the rest of Scotland, and it has been estimated that the annual profit was around £18,000.

Yet we find Duncan Forbes, in the Culloden papers, writing on the subject of the Excise:

The imminent distress, from the condition of our Revenue, has now for some time possessed my attention; the Customs, from the defects of the Law, from the corruption of the officers, and from the perverseness of juries, are fallen to nothing; and never can by any art be raised, till these complaints are removed, which must be the work of some time, though our disease seems to require a more speedy remedy.

The Excise, though not under so correct management as formerly, seems to be the only revenue from which we can look for any immediate relief, but unless it is put on a better foot, we cannot depend upon its answering any immediate purpose.

The reason for this he ascribed to the enormous quantities of foreign brandy being smuggled into the country. In 1730 he succeeded in passing a resolution against foreign spirit drinking at the Convention of Royal Burghs. The intention was to make the drinking of foreign spirits illegal, but, hardly surprisingly, it was not put into effect. The suggestion that he might give up his privilege and thus increase the revenue considerably does not seem to have been put to him, although it undoubtedly caused considerable resentment among other distillers and the subject was raised in Parliament. The argument was put forward that he had been granted a virtual monopoly and that the losses he had suffered were no more than a year's rent, but for the moment nothing came of these objections. Lord President Forbes was too strong a supporter of the English and the Union to be lightly cast aside.

As Duncan Forbes's record shows, the enforcement of the Excise was extremely lax and corrupt and smuggling was an accepted facet of life which no-one condemned strongly, since from the highest to the lowest in the land there was no-one who would readily refuse smuggled goods when offered them. Yet in Scotland discontent with rule from the south and the heavy rate of taxation, particularly the malt tax, was still extremely strong. The famous Porteous Riot in Edinburgh in 1736 made this plain enough, although ostensibly concerned with the events following the hanging of a smuggler named Wilson.

Wilson and a companion Robertson had been condemned to death for stealing £200 from the Customs House at Pittenweem where their smuggled goods had been held after seizure. Wilson, blaming himself for his younger friend's sentence, ensured his escape from St. Giles where they were attending service under guard by a remarkable feat of strength. Allan Ramsay, the painter and poet, described the event in a letter to Duncan Forbes:

Wilson, who was a very strong fellow, took Robertson by the head band of his breeks and threw him out of his seat, held a soger fast in each hand and one of them with his teeth, while Robertson got over and through the pews, pushed o'er the elder and plate at the door, made his way through Parliament close, down the back stair, got out of the poteraw gate before it was shut, the mob making way and fairly assisting him, got friends, money, and a swift horse and fairly got off, nae mair to be heard of or seen.

There was considerable sympathy with Wilson and a large crowd attended his hanging which was supervised, as customary, by the City Guard commanded by a Captain Porteous. All went quietly until the hanging was over when stones were thrown at the Guard. Porteous panicked and ordered his men to fire over the heads of the crowd. Several spectators at upstairs windows were killed or wounded and the temper of the mob grew extremely ugly so that Porteous was forced to order his men to fire again. In the end three men, a woman and a boy were killed and several others wounded.

Porteous was put on trial, convicted and condemned to death, but a stay of execution was granted by the intervention of the Queen, first step in a reprieve. On hearing the news a mob gathered in the Grassmarket, overwhelmed the City Guard and stormed the prison. Removing Porteous from his cell, they hanged him in the customary place of execution. They then dispersed quietly. The obvious organisation behind the lynching enraged the government in the south and a bill was tabled with a view to imprisoning the Provost of Edinburgh. Ultimately, after considerable emendation, less drastic action was taken. The Provost was deprived of the office of magistrate and a fine of £2,000 was imposed on the city for Porteous's widow.

The same year, 1736, saw the magistrates of Middlesex petitioning Parliament:

That the drinking of Geneva, and other distilled liquors had for some years greatly increased: That the constant and excessive use thereof had destroyed thousands of his Majesty's subjects: That great numbers of others were by its use rendered unfit for useful labour, debauched in morals, and drawn into all manner of vice and wickedness. . . .

The result was the passing of the notorious Gin Act later in the year.

An earlier attempt to control the evil effects of excessive gin drinking in the south, an Act of 1729, had introduced a licence for retailers and a tax on gin, but had been easily evaded. A further Act in 1733 aimed at reducing the number of spirit shops had prevented the sale of spirits outside dwelling houses, thus giving a free licence to any dwelling house. The 1736 Act, specifically exempting

Scotland from its provisions, raised the duty on spirits to £1 a gallon and the price of a retail licence to £50. The immediate effect was considerable rioting in London and subsequently widespread evasion, since it merely had the effect of causing the retailers to flout the law openly by peddling gin in the guise of patent medicines with names such as 'My Lady's Eye Water', 'The Cure for Blue Devils', and 'Old Tom'.

As Lord Carteret said in the House of Lords:

Since the populace saw that they could not evade the law, they openly and avowedly transgressed it; and the transgressors were so numerous that they set the Government itself at defiance. No private man, no under officer durst inform, no magistrate durst punish, without being in danger of . . . the mob as he passed along the streets.

Smollett's description of this period, written about 1760, bears repetition:

Such a shameful degree of pofligacy prevailed that the retailers of this poisonous compound set up printed boards in public inviting people to be drunk for the small expense of one penny, assuring them that they might be dead drunk for twopence and have straw for nothing. They accordingly provided cellars and places strewed with straw, to which they conveyed the wretches who were overwhelmed with intoxication. In these dismal caverns they lay until they recovered some use of their faculties and then they had recourse to the same mischievous compound.

Estimates of the vast amounts of spirits consumed during this period vary wildly, from around eight million gallons annually to as much as double that figure. Since this does not of course include illegally distilled spirits, or spirits smuggled into the country, the amount consumed must be anyone's guess. The fact that only two distillers took out licences in the seven years following the Act of 1736 speaks for itself. It was not until 1742, when the 1736 Act was repealed and the magistrates were given more powers in the matter of granting licences, that the legislation began to have effect.

Wise after the event, Lord Islay summed it up in the debate in 1742 when he said: 'Every man . . . foresaw that it was such a law as could not be executed, but as the poor had run gin-mad, the rich had run anti-gin-mad, and in this fit of madness no one would give an ear to reason.'

In 1743 France joined Spain against Britain in the War of the Austrian Succession and the hopes of the Jacobites in the north began to rise once more with the news that Prince Charles Edward Stuart, the Young Pretender, son of the Old Pretender, had rallied French support to his cause. The appearance of a

British Fleet and a violent storm in February 1744 combined to disperse the French invasion force of troopships and proved enough for them. The young Prince was unable to obtain any further French backing and impetuously announced his intention of sailing to Scotland in 1745. Faced with sudden reality, his supporters attempted to dissuade him, but their warnings never reached him. On 23rd July 1745 with a mere nine companions, of whom only three were Scots, he landed at Eriskay in the Outer Hebrides.

Despite the seeming impossibility of the attempt many of the Highland chieftains rallied to him. The memory of Glencoe combined with a distrust and dislike of the government in the south, of the payment of Excise duties and of such measures as the Disarming Act, as much as any deep-seated loyalty for the Stuarts, were behind their decision. It is hard to blame them in retrospect. The young, handsome Prince had considerable charm and a persuasive tongue and it is not easy to keep a cool head in the magic atmosphere of the Western Highlands. The Jacobite Standard was raised at Glenfinnan on the 19th of August.

On the 16th of September Edinburgh was taken without bloodshed. On the 20th the Highlanders had defeated the raw government forces under Sir John Cope at Prestonpans. After a pause to recruit his forces Charles marched south. On the 15th of November he captured Carlisle without firing a shot. By the 3rd of December he had reached Derby and there was panic in London with the Bank of England forced to pay out in sixpences, but this was the limit of his penetration south. By Christmas day he was back in Glasgow and, although the Highlanders were to win a further victory at the Battle of Falkirk, it was clear that Charles had lost heart. In April 1746 came Culloden and the end of his hopes. It was also the death knell of the old Highland way of life.

The full fury of a badly frightened Parliament in the south was unleashed against the defeated Highlanders. 'Butcher' Cumberland earned his nickname well from the murder, rapine and looting which followed on his victory, for the hunting down of Jacobites and the fugitive Prince resulted in months of terror throughout the Highlands. Then came savage reprisals, the banning of all weapons, the outlawing of the Highland dress, the garrisoning of the Highland fortresses. For over three decades the Highlands were subjected to harsh repression of this nature. Small wonder if they turned increasingly to whisky for comfort.

During his five months, from April to September, of fugitive wanderings through the Highlands and Islands, Charles proved himself no mean whisky drinker and he seems to have thrived on it. The Rev. John Cameron described him unromantically at one point as 'bare footed, had an old black kilt coat on, philabeg [i.e., kilt] and waistcoat, a dirty shirt and a long red beard, a gun in his hand, a pistol and dirk by his side. He was very cheerful and in good health and in my opinion fatter than when he was in Inverness'.

By the time he had reached the temporary safety of South Uist he appears to have acquired 'tartan hose and Highland brogues'. There he had a drinking session with Macdonald of Boisdale and Macdonald of Baleshare which the latter described thus:

He called a dram, being the first article of Highland entertainment, which, being over, he called for meat. There was half a stone of butter laid on a timber plate, and near a leg of beef laid on a patch before us. . . . The Young Gentleman told us, as it was seldom he met friends he could enjoy himself with, he would on no account part with us that night. Boisdale says to me that we could not in good manners part with him that night. . . . The Young Gentleman advises Edward Burke to fill the bowl. Boisdale insists on his being shaved first and then putting on a clean shirt. Then we began with our bowl frank and free. As we were turning merry, we were turning more free. . . . We continued this drinking for three days and nights. He still had the better of us, even of Boisdale himself, notwithstanding his being as able a bowlsman, I daresay, as any in Scotland.

Disguised improbably as Flora Macdonald's serving wench in a 'flowered linen gown, a light coloured quilted petticoat, and a mantle of dun camlet, made after the Irish fashion with a hood', Charles made good his escape to Skye. There he had an evening's drinking with Macdonald of Kingsburgh, ending by breaking his host's china punchbowl from which they had been drinking whisky toddy. Reverting to kilt and plaid he left Portree with a whisky bottle tied to his belt, finally leaving from the mainland in the French ship *L'Heureux*. Behind him he left the Highlands which were never to be the same again, where years of misery and distress were only ultimately to be alleviated by wholesale emigration.

Among the many fugitives in the Highlands at this time was a certain John Gow, who had been out both in the rising of 1715 and that of 1745. Finding his old haunts near Braemar too hot for comfort he fled over the Ladder, the whisky smugglers' track in the hills, to the wild countryside in Glenlivet near Tomintoul. To secure himself from undue inquisitiveness about his past he changed his name, anglicising the Gaelic Gow to Smith. As John Smith he settled down with his wife and family in the Tomintoul Glenlivet area with only Highlanders of the same old religion round him, to farm and distil his own whisky. In that wild area he seems to have succeeded in living peacefully without undue disturbance from the English soldiery.

The subjugation of the Highlands was thorough, but undoubtedly more severe in some parts than others. The rough and ready methods of supervision adopted by some of the English garrisons may be gauged from the doubtful advice given to his subordinates by Lieutenant Colonel Watson commanding Fort Augustus in 1747. He wrote:

How soon the posts are fixed the commanding officer at each station is to endeavour to ingratiate himself in the favour of some person in his neighbourhood by giving him a reward, or filling him drunk with whisky as often as he may judge proper, which I'm confident is the only way to penetrate the secrets of these people.

Everything passes with time, however, and over the years the more irksome restrictions in the Highlands were gradually eased. In the same way over the years the government finally succeeded in reducing the consumption of gin in England. The Act of 1750, by which time consumption was reckoned to be well over eight million gallons a year, began to take effect and the amending Act of 1751 completed the process. By the year 1758 consumption had dropped to near two million gallons annually.

By 1756, when the Seven Years' War with France began, no doubt the restrictions in the Highlands had already eased somewhat. Many of the Highlanders, eager to bear arms and wear Highland dress, had already joined Highland regiments as the only means open to them of doing so. It did not take the government long to appreciate that here was a way to channel the Highlander's warlike instincts in their own interests. Between 1740 and 1815 no less than eighty-six Highland regiments were raised in defence of Britain. They were soon famous for their ardour in battle. As Robert Burns was to put it:

> But bring a Scotsman frae his hill,
> Clap in his cheek a Highland gill,
> Say, such is Royal George's will,
> An' there's the foe:
> He has nae thought but how to kill
> Twa at a blow.

THE

Diſtillery of SCOTLAND

A

NATIONAL BENEFIT;

AND

The IMPORTATION and USE of
FOREIGN SPIRITS,

A

NATIONAL DETRIMENT

DEMONSTRATE

In a LETTER to a FRIEND.

ABERDEEN:

Printed by J. CHALMERS, and ſold by R. FARQUHAR.

M.DCC.LV.

In 1760, with the British army victorious in the field as seldom before, George II died. He was succeeded by his grandson, the 22-year-old George III, still very much under the influence of 'his dear friend' and old tutor, the Earl of Bute, First Lord of the Treasury and reputedly also the Queen's lover. He was by no means the only Scot in an influential position at court. The Adam brothers were court architects, Ramsay was court painter. There were many other Scots, in the government, in the army, navy and official positions of power, as well as merchants and bankers of wealth and influence in the City.

By this time certain effects of the Union were becoming obvious. With the advent of new agricultural methods from the south, farming was already improving in the Lowlands. At the same time the erstwhile flourishing Firth of Forth mercantile ports were falling into decay because of the decrease in direct trade with the Continent. In the north Wade's roads had successfully opened up the Highlands and many Highlanders were taking advantage of them to emigrate to England. More and more Scots were moving south.

With memories still strong of their fears during the 1745 rebellion, the English masses bitterly resented the influx. The fact that many Scots took posts as Gaugers and Excise officials merely intensified feeling against them in the same way that dislike of the English Gaugers and Excise officials had been strong in Scotland soon after the Union. The resentment against Bute, as the power behind the throne, was particularly widespread and these sentiments were fanned by John Wilkes in his scurrilous magazine *The North Briton*. During the Wilkes Riots of 1763 anti-Scots feeling was particularly high and such prejudices did not easily fade.

As late as 1773 Johnson had to be persuaded by Boswell that it was quite unnecessary for him to arm himself with a pair of pistols before leaving for a tour of the Highlands. He was soon, however, agreeably surprised and wrote: 'Civility seems part of the natural character of the Highlands'. On reaching Skye he expounded at some length:

A man of the Hebrides, for of the women's diet I can give no account, as soon as he appears in the morning, swallows a glass of whisky; yet they are not a drunken race, at least I never was present at much intemperance; but no man is so abstemious as to refuse a morning dram, which they call a *skalk*.

The word *whisky* signifies water, and is applied by way of eminence to *strong water*, or distilled liquor. The spirit drunk in the north is drawn from barley. I never tasted it, except once for experiment at the inn at Inverary, when I thought it preferable to any

English malt brandy. It was strong, but not pungent, and was free from the empyreumatick taste or smell. What was the process I had no opportunity of inquiring, nor do I wish to improve the art of making poison pleasant.

Not long after the dram may be expected the breakfast. . . .

While visiting the island of Coll, Boswell noted that they drank whisky out of a shell 'according to the ancient Highland custom'. Johnson recorded:

The *malt tax* for Col is twenty shillings. Whisky is very plentiful; there are several stills on the Island, and more is made than the inhabitants consume.

When they were at Inveraray Boswell recorded the occasion when Dr. Johnson drank some whisky as follows:

We supped well; and after supper, Dr. Johnson, whom I had not seen taste any fermented liquor during all our travels, called for a gill of whisky. 'Come (said he), let me know what it is that makes a Scotchman happy!' He drank it all but a drop, which I begged leave to pour into my glass, that I might say we had drunk whisky together. . . .

Another early traveller in the Highlands was the eccentric Yorkshire sporting squire, Colonel Thomas Thornton, who had been educated at Glasgow University in 1766 and frequently visited the country thereafter. The forerunner of countless sporting English visitors in the 19th century, Thornton wrote a book based on his journeys, supposedly dated 1784, but really the product of many different years. A confirmed Scotophil he was immensely wealthy and travelled with his own supplies of wine, rum and 'incomparable porter from Calverts'; hence, as a consequence, he does not seem to have drunk a great deal of whisky, though he refers to it at one point as 'the darling liquor of the country'.

In the year 1784 one notable event in the history of the whisky industry occurred. After complaints had mounted over the years, the Forbeses' exemption from Excise duty was finally withdrawn. An Act was duly passed:

Whereas Arthur Forbes of Culloden Esq., in the county of Inverness, is possessed of an exemption from the duties of Excise, within the lands of Ferintosh, under several Acts of Parliament of Scotland, which exemption has been found detrimental to the revenue and to the distillery in other parts of Scotland enacted that the Treasury shall agree with the said Arthur Forbes upon a compensation to be paid to him in lieu of the exemption and if they shall not agree, the Barons of Exchequer may settle the compensation by a jury, and after payment thereof, the said exemption shall cease.

50

A grant of a further £21,000 in compensation was finally paid. All things considered, the Forbeses had done very well out of the raid in 1688 and the damage to their distillery at Ferintosh. It was left to Burns to immortalise the event with the mildly satirical verse poking fun at 'loyal Forbes' charter'd boast', quoted at the start of this chapter.

5. Riots in Leith 1784 to General Stewart of Garth on 1814 Act

They cursed horse leeches o' th'excise,
Who mak the whisky stells their prize!
Haud up thy han', Deil! ance, twice, thrice!
There, seize the blinkers;
An' bake them up in brunstane pies
For poor damnd drinkers.

Scotch Drink, ROBERT BURNS 1786

Although most of the Scots whisky distillers used stills of a capacity from ten to eighty gallons there were already by the 1770s some large Lowland distillers with stills capable of distilling a thousand gallons at a time. These, of course, were licensed distillers and by this time already sending their product south,

52

even if only to be turned into gin. It should be appreciated, however, that illicit distilling was by no means confined to the Highlands for in 1777 it was said that there were eight licensed distillers in Edinburgh and four hundred illicit stills.

During his visit to Scotland in 1784 Colonel Thomas Thornton mentioned a friend of his in the King's Own Dragoons, a Captain Sykes, being involved in riots. According to the *Edinburgh Weekly Review*, on the evening of the 4th of June Mr. Haig's distillery at Leith had been attacked by a mob who were convinced that the distillery was using supplies of oats and other grain, potatoes and root crops for distilling, thus causing a shortage in the markets. Two men left as night watchmen opened fire and a rioter was killed. The riot then grew serious and the troops were called out to quell it, behaving, according to the report, with admirable restraint and taking the two watchmen into custody for their own protection.

Three days later there was another riot at the distillery and the troops were again called out. The matter was apparently finally settled by Mr. Haig paying compensation to the family of the man who had been killed. He was also forced to issue a statement in his own defence, denying that there was any foundation for the rumours that he used foodstuffs such as grain and potatoes for distilling. His statement ran:

It has unhappily taken possession of the minds of many people that all sorts of grain, wheat, oats, barley and pease, are there consumed in great quantities, and that even oat-meal and roots, such as potatoes, turnips, and carrots are made to serve the purposes of distillation; and, consequently that the markets are affected by this supposed consumption. Now, the genuine truth is, that no other species of grain are made use of at the Canonmills but barley, rye, and sometimes such parcels of wheat as happen to receive damage, or are in quality unfit for bread; and that not a grain of oats, pease, or a particle of oat-meal, not any potatoes, carrots, turnips, or other roots, are used in the distillery in any shape.

The fact that Mr. Haig specifically referred only to his own distillery is probably significant, since some distilleries in the Lowlands undoubtedly used oats and potatoes, as well as the inferior wheat and unmalted grain he admitted to using occasionally. His, of course, was one of the largest licensed distilleries in the Lowlands and a good part of his spirit was sent to England. Since it would then, in any event, be re-distilled and rectified into gin, the use of such methods was relatively unimportant. It is understandable, however, that very often the whisky produced illicitly in the Highlands was preferable to this type of spirit.

The methods used by the illicit distillers in the Highlands were comparatively simple, but nonetheless effective. Unless the local Gauger was corrupt, which seems more often than not to have been the case, the still itself would usually be situated in an out-of-the-way glen where it was unlikely to be discovered. The Highland method of taking grazing cattle up into the hills in the spring and living with them in a shieling, or temporary hut, often surviving on blood drawn from the cattle themselves mixed with oatmeal, lent itself to illicit distilling. Then a still could be built in the security of the mountains near a convenient burn and all the preparations made without fear of interruption.

The sacks of barley would be steeped for two days or so in a burn or bog before being laid out to germinate either in a barn or, more probably, in a convenient cave in the hillside. For the next ten days or so the barley would be turned every day until it had reached what was judged to be a suitable state of germination. Then it would be dried over a peat fire to check the growth.

The malted grains would next be tipped into the mash-tun, often an open barrel with heather lining the bottom. The malted barley would then have boiling water poured over it and the mixture would be stirred for a couple of hours before the resulting worts were drained off with the heather acting as a filter. The process would be repeated with the same grains a second time and the resulting wort would be mixed in a larger barrel and allowed to ferment with the addition of some yeast.

Within a day or two the resulting wash would be ready to put through the still to turn into low wines. Since there was generally only the one still in an illicit distillery of this nature, the entire still had to be carefully cleaned before the resulting low wines could be put through it again. If this was not done the spirits produced by the second distillation would inevitably have a strong, unpleasantly smoky flavour.

The still itself might vary from a cauldron with a head, or cover and spout, fitting over it like a lid, tightly sealed with tow, to a specially built copper still of upright shape. The head would lead off into the worm, or coil, which was often enclosed in a barrel through which running water was led from the burn. The junction of head and coil was also probably sealed with tow to ensure a tight fit. The coil itself might be made of lead or copper, but, according to Joseph Mitchell in his *Reminiscences* about the turn of the century, 'so general was smuggling that at Inverness there were two or three master coppersmiths who had a sign above their shops of a whisky still, indicating their employment'.

The skill and experience in the distilling lay in knowing when to draw off the pure middle run of spirit, avoiding the oily higher alcohols, or foreshots, at the start and the later lower alcohols, or tailings, both of which could be kept for later redistillation. Although it may sound a complicated enough business, there is no doubt that over the centuries the Highland distillers had reduced it to a fine art, which they thoroughly understood. By the mid-18th century it is equally certain that many of the more permanent illicit stills were producing much better whisky than their licensed opposite numbers simply because the latter were forced by the malt tax to use unmalted grain in addition to their malt to make their product economic.

Burt's description of his encounter with some 'usky merchants' in the Highlands was a scene which might have been witnessed at any time in the Highlands well into the 19th century. Almost certainly they were illicit distillers taking their goods south for sale. He wrote:

I was at length stopped by a small river that was become impassable. There happened, luckily for me, to be a public hut in this place . . . but there was nothing to drink. . . . In about three hours after my arrival at this hut, there appeared on the other side of the water a parcel of merchants, with little horses loaded with roundlets of usky.

Within sight of the ford was a bridge (as they called it) made for the convenience of this place. It was composed of two small fir-trees not squared at all, laid one beside the other, across a narrow part of the river, from rock to rock. There were gaps and intervals between those trees and beneath a most tumultuous fall of water.

Some of my merchants bestriding the bridge edged forwards and moved the usky vessels before them; but the others to my surprise walked over this dangerous passage, and dragged their *garrons* through the torrent, while the poor little horses were almost drowned with the surge.

I happened to have a few lemons left, and with them I so far qualified the ill taste of the spirit as to make it tolerable. . . . The usky men were my companions, whom it was expected I should treat according to custom; there being no partition to separate them from me. And thus I passed a part of the day, and great part of the night in the smoke and dreading the bed.

Since at that time the principle of keeping the spirit in the cask for any length of time to mature had not been evolved, there seems little doubt that Captain Burt was drinking whisky almost straight from the still. It says a great deal for it in the circumstances that it was drinkable, even with lemons added to it. This must have been more than could be said for a great deal of the spirit distilled in the Lowlands with the addition of wheat, oats, rye or potatoes to the malted grain, even if that was only intended for the English market to be re-distilled and rectified into gin. Such a spirit was not whisky even though distilled in larger quantities and under better circumstances than the illicit Highland 'usky'.

The 'parcel of merchants' seen by Burt, were almost certainly, of course, smugglers. His carelessness as to whether wine or spirits had paid duty or not was typical of the general attitude throughout the 18th century. At one point on his journeys in 1784, while near Lanark, Colonel Thornton, though himself a magistrate, demonstrated the same careless attitude of the otherwise law-abiding citizen of the day towards smuggling. He wrote:

As I passed, we saw a tribe of gentry, whom I took to be smugglers, and, being in good spirits, I gave them to understand that some custom-house officers were behind in search of them. They thanked me for my hint, and availed themselves of it, by leaving the road instantly, which confirmed my suspicions, and I thought they unloaded their goods on the moors; but the day turning foggy, we soon lost sight of them.

The year 1784 was a bad one for the Scots whisky distillers. In that year, due to continual pressure and complaints from the English distillers about the favourable rate of taxation in Scotland, Pitt the Younger's government finally introduced what was known as the Wash Act. This was intended to remedy what was regarded as unfair competition in the south from increasing quantities of Scots spirits being produced at a lower tax rate. By this Act, for the first time, a clear distinction was drawn between Highlands and Lowlands. The boundary thus defined by Act of Parliament ran:

A certain line or boundary beginning at the east point of Loch Crinan, and proceeding from thence to Loch Gilpin; from thence . . . along the west side of Loch Fyne, to Inveraray and to the head of Loch Fyne; from thence . . . to Arrochar . . . to Tarbet; from Tarbet in a supposed line straight eastward on the north side of Ben Lomond, to . . . Callander . . . from thence north eastward to Crieff . . . to Ambleree [Amulree] and Inver to Dunkeld; from thence along the foot and side of the Grampian Hills to Fettercairn . . . and from thence northward . . . to . . . Kincardine O'Neil, Clatt, Huntly and Keith to Fochabers; and from thence westward by Elgin and Forres, to the boat on the river Findhorn, and from thence down the said river to the sea at Findhorn, and any place in or part of the county of Elgin which lies southward of the said line from Fochabers to the sea at Findhorn.

By the Wash Act the Highland distillers were required to pay an annual licence of 20s per gallon based on the capacity of the still. The Lowland distilleries, most unfairly, were taxed at the English rate of 5d per gallon of wash, on the mistaken governmental assumption that so much wash must produce so much spirit, both in England and Scotland. The government considered a tax on this basis fair and reasonable, but failed completely to appreciate the great difference in the specific gravities of the wash in Scotland compared with that of England. The wash in England was artificially saccharified and of a much higher gravity intended for making gin. The gravity of the Scots wash for whisky was much lower since much less spirit was produced from it, but this was intended for consumption without re-distilling as was the case in England. The injustice of the tax was soon plain and in 1786 it was changed to an annual licence based on the still content.

The Distillery Act of 1786 made no distinction between Highlands and Lowlands. By this Act an annual licence of £1.10s per gallon of still content was imposed, which was estimated as working out at 6d per gallon of whisky produced. The Act also added an extra 2s per gallon on whisky imported into England to equal the English duty of 2s 6d per gallon on spirits. By this means the government hoped to equalise Scots and English duties, but once again they failed to appreciate the rudiments of what was involved.

There were two basic snags to the 1786 Act. Firstly, it quite naturally gave a tremendous impetus to smuggling of spirits into England, since the smuggler stood to gain considerably. Secondly, it made the basic error of assuming that a still could only be worked once in twenty-four hours and it was on this assumption that the duty was estimated. This fundamental flaw in the Act at once set Scots ingenuity to devising new shapes and types of still which could be worked faster and more efficiently. It was, indeed, as a result of this Act and its successors that the modern shape of still was evolved.

By 1788 the baffled government discovered that it had underestimated the amount of whisky which could be distilled within twenty-four hours, as to its surprise and the dismay of the English distillers the imports to England continued to increase apace. Accordingly a further 6d duty per gallon was added to the Scots spirits sent to England, although English duty remained at 2s 6d. An Act was also passed doubling the licence duty per gallon of still content to £3.

Meanwhile Boyle's hydrometer, originally designed for detecting counterfeit coin rather than measuring proof strength; although adapted by the Excise for revenue purposes, had proved inadequate. Finally a Mr. Clarke produced a new design for a hydrometer made of copper, described as: '. . . having a brass wire about 1 in. thick going through and soldered into the copper ball. . . . There are two . . . marks "A" and "B" . . . to show whether the liquor be 1/10th above proof . . . or 1/10th under proof . . . when a brass weight such as "C" has been screwed on to the bottom. . . . There are a great many such weights of different sizes. . . .' Although Clarke's hydrometer was officially adopted by the Excise in 1787, it was decidedly erratic in use. A clear definition of 'proof' was still not feasible.

Not unnaturally these alterations, the introduction of the new hydrometer and the tax changes, had no effect on the illicit distillers who were not paying any tax anyway, but they did have a considerable effect on the large distillers in the Lowlands. Among these the most prominent were the brothers James and John Haig at Leith, already mentioned, and James and John Stein in Clackmannanshire, who had large distilleries at Kilbagie and Kennetpans. The Haig brothers managed to survive this increase in duty, although undoubtedly hard hit by it. The Stein brothers, who had begun to rely increasingly on importing spirits to the English market and were engaged in a price war with the southern distillers, were immediately forced into bankruptcy. The English distillers promptly, and no doubt with relief, raised their prices. There is little doubt that the wealthy and powerful distillers' lobby in England had successfully pressed for this discriminatory protective legislation, which virtually put an end to imports of whisky from Scotland as being uneconomic. Naturally, however, the immediate effect was an increase in smuggling once more.

Describing the Steins' distilleries for the *Statistical Account of Scotland* a few years later, the Rev. Robert Moody noted with obvious regret:

Previous to the year 1788 the quantity of corn used annually at the distillery at Kilbagie alone, amounted to above 60,000 bolls, and the annual quantity of spirits made, to above 3,000 tons. The black cattle fed annually were about 7,000; swine 2,000. The cattle were sold to butchers, who drove them to Edinburgh and Glasgow markets; the swine were killed and cured into bacon and pork for England. The work people employed were nearly 300. The distillery and utensils cost upwards of 40,000l Sterling; and when sold by the trustee for the creditors of the former proprietors, yielded about 7,000l Sterling.

No situation could have been more eligible for a distillery than Kilbagie and it was erected in the most substantial manner. The buildings occupy a space of above 4 acres of ground; all surrounded by a high wall. The barns for malting are of a prodigious size, and are 4 stories in height. A small rivulet runs through the middle of the works and drives a threshing mill, and all the grinding mills necessary for the distillery; besides supplying with water a canal, which communicates with the river Forth, of about a mile in length, cut for the purpose of conveying both the imports and exports of the distillery.

The distillery at Kennetpans, which is advantageously situated on the very banks of the river Forth, was in proportion to that of Kilbagie, as three to five. And before these two distilleries were stopped, they paid the government an excise duty considerably greater than the whole land tax of Scotland.

In the same year that the Steins were forced into bankruptcy, Robert Burns, aged 29, took a step about which he himself had grave misgivings. He wrote to his friend Miss Chalmers on February 17th 1788: 'I have altered all my plans of future life. A farm that I could live in, I could not find. . . . You will condemn me for the next step I have taken; I have entered the Excise. . . .' He found his farm at Ellisland in Dumfriesshire the same year and prepared for marriage. Four years later, as a fully fledged Excise officer he was to write the famous verses which typified public feeling for his service:

> The deil cam fiddling thro' the town,
> And danc'd awa' wi' th'Exciseman:
> And ilka wife cries, auld Mahoun,
> I wish you luck o' the prize, man.

> We'll mak our maut, and we'll brew our drink,
> We'll laugh, sing, and rejoice, man;
> And mony braw thanks to the meikle black deil,
> That danc'd awa' wi' th'Exciseman.

The outbreak of the French Revolution in 1789 made little difference to Scotland, unless it brought a shade more disregard for authority with it. Throughout the Highlands and a large part of the Lowlands illicit distilling continued in almost open defiance of the law. The clergymen and church in general did not always set a particularly good example.

As far back as 1741, for instance, when Excisemen in Southwick, Kirkcudbrightshire, seized goods belonging to a William Lindsay he returned with some friends on the sabbath and attacked them. Hailed before the Kirk Session for sabbath breaking, he and his friends admitted to it, but requested that their rebuke should be kept private so as not to assist the Excise officers in their case, and this was duly agreed. In 1754 the Rev. Aeneas Macauley of Gairloch was accused by his synod of buying supplies of smuggled rum and geneva and selling them to his parishioners.

59

One of the most notorious smugglers in Kirkwall, Orkney, was Magnus Eunson, a United Presbyterian Church officer, who frequently stored smuggled whisky under the pulpit of his church. Learning of a raid being planned on the church on one occasion he transferred the barrels to his house and covered them with a coffin and a white cloth to look like a bier. When the Excisemen arrived they found his entire family kneeling round the 'corpse' in prayer. A mention of smallpox was enough to send them on their way.

On the whole it was rare for ministers to be actively involved in smuggling, but in common with the rest of the country they were generally prepared to turn a blind eye to what went on around them and were willing enough to accept smuggled goods if offered to them cheaply enough. Typical perhaps was the Rev. Mr. John Grant's attitude to his flock at Tomintoul, above the famed Glenlivet area, where in 1790, when he was writing in the *First Statistical Account*, there were some two hundred illicit stills. He recorded:

Tammtoul . . . is inhabited by 37 families, without a single manufacture. . . . All of them sell whisky and all of them drink it. When disengaged from this business the women spin yarn, kiss their innamoratos, or dance to the discordant strains of an old fiddle. . . . Here the Roman Catholic Priest has got an elegant meeting-house, and the Protestant clergyman the reverse. . . . A school is stationed at this village attended by 40 or 50 little recreants all promising to be very like their parents.

This was probably the school to which the erstwhile John Gow, alias John Smith, had sent his son Andrew after moving to this area in 1747. It was almost certainly here that George Smith, his grandson, born in 1792, received his initial education before going on to train as a builder and architect. It was very probably in this village school that he gained his grounding in Latin. By this time the Smiths were respectable farmers, farming the Upper Drumin holding in Glenlivet and, naturally, in those surroundings, distilling illicitly at the same time. Such practices were absolutely necessary in order to pay their rent, since the price of corn by itself was insufficient to do so. Transformed into whisky, however, it provided enough to live on as well.

This was a point made by many ministers and others writing in the *First Statistical Account of Scotland*. An example is the comment of the Rev. Mr. John Downie of Urray, in the Presbytery of Dingwall, writing in 1793:

. . . No doubt such a number engaged in distilling spirits, has a tendency to corrupt the morals; but the bad effects of this trade are less discernible than might be feared.

Were the effects worse than they are, there is a fatal necessity of continuing the distillery, until some other manufacture be established in its stead, whereby the people will be enabled to find money to pay their rents. . . .

The outbreak of war with France in 1793 resulted in the licence duty being trebled to £9. Once again the ingenuity of the distillers was exercised in producing yet quicker distillation, and once again they succeeded. The stage was reached where eighty-gallon stills were being worked off in three and a half minutes. The distiller thus absorbed the increased tax at the expense of wearing out the still and producing inferior whisky, since inevitably quality suffered in such speedy distilling. Inevitably also illicit distilling increased.

Certainly there seems to have been little check in the output of whisky and merchants were increasingly finding it worth their while to set up in the trade as middlemen. One such wine and spirit merchant who set up in this year, 1793, in Rose Street in Edinburgh was a certain William Hill, the forerunner of many others. Apparently finding the war no impediment to his trade, within six years he had moved to a handsome Georgian house at 45, Frederick Street, training his sons to succeed him. Since there cannot have been a great trade in wine during the war, it must be assumed that he dealt principally in whisky from the start, for by this time whisky was by far the most popular drink in Scotland.

The prevalence of distilling, both licensed and illicit, is mirrored in the many references to it in the *First Statistical Account*. Writing in 1794, the Rev. Mr. John Smith made the point that it could be considered desirable to raise the tax even further to a prohibitive level, but he foresaw clearly the results if this were done. After noting the thirty-two licensed distilleries in the town and surrounding country, he wrote:

This business is undoubtedly gainful to a few individuals, but extremely ruinous to the community. It consumes their means, hurts their morals, and destroys both their undertakings and their health. Were it not for preventing the temptation of smuggling, a duty next to prohibition would be a mercy. . . .

Despite his obvious bias against whisky he pointed out the disadvantages of the heavy excise duty which made exporting to England uneconomic. He continued:

. . . the prospect of enormous gain, first tempts the indigent to convert their crop into a pernicious liquor, and then the law obliges them to drink it themselves, as it cannot be sold but where they have equal poverty and equal liberty. Thus, in the trite story, two publicans, who went alternately to each others houses, with the same twopence, drank both their cellars dry. Were we allowed to export a part, to help us pay our meal and flour, it would do us much service. . . .

In 1795 the government doubled the licence duty yet again to £18. Even this failed to discourage the whisky distillers, who merely redoubled their efforts to beat the tax. New sizes and shapes of stills were continually being tried out and some of them were proving successful. Inevitably, however, many reverted to illicit distilling as their only solution to the problem.

The Rev. Mr. David Dunoon, writing in the *Statistical Account* for his parish of Killearnan in Ross-shire in 1796, ended his description of the extensive distilling there by indicating the reasons for it. Somewhat drily he recorded:

Distilling is almost the only method of converting our victual into cash for the payment of rent and servants; and whisky may, in fact, be called our staple commodity. The distillers do not lay the proper value on their time and trouble, and of course look on all, but the price of barley and the fire added to the tax, as clear profit; add to these the luxury of tasting the quality of manufacture during the process.

The following year the licence duty was increased yet again to an unheard-of £54. By this time many stills were being operated continuously in an effort to beat the rate of taxation. The fact that the stills were being rapidly worn out in the process seems to have been accepted as part of the price they had to pay. The effects, however, were that the richer and larger distillers were the ones who profited most by the increase in taxation. The smaller man was being heavily penalised, or else being forced to distil illegally.

When a Committee on Distilleries was set up by the government in 1798 to try to solve the problem, John Stein, who had owned the distilleries in Clackmannanshire forced into bankruptcy in 1788, gave evidence on distilling as follows:

It is not confined to great towns or regular manufacturers, but spreads itself over the whole face of the country, and in every island from the Orkneys to Jura. There are many who practice this art who are ignorant of every other, and there are distillers who boast that they make the best possible whiskey, who cannot read or write, and who carry on this manufacture in parts of the country where the use of the plough is unknown and where the face of the Exciseman is never seen. Under such circumstances, it is impossible to take account of its operations, it is literally to search for revenue in the woods or on the mountains.

I Titlepage of Hieronymous Braunschweig's treatise on distilling (1519)

II A 16th-century still house

III Alchemists at work in the 17th century

IV Stoking the kiln in the 17th century

V Stoking the still in a modern still house

Dr. John Leyden in his *Journal of a Tour to the Highlands in 1800* noted the economic factors and their effects disapprovingly:

The distillation of whiskey presents an irresistible temptation to the poorer classes, as the boll of barley, which costs thirty shillings, produces by this process, between five and six guineas. This distillation had a most ruinous effect in increasing the scarcity of grain last year, particularly in Isla and Tiree, where the people subsisted chiefly on fish and potatoes.

The government could think of no better solution than to double the tax from £54 to £108 in the year 1800. This was bad enough and putting an intolerable strain on the smaller distillers, but, following the short-lived Treaty of Amiens in 1802, when war broke out again in 1803 they raised the tax yet once more to £162. Inevitably this merely increased illicit distilling and smuggling to unprecedented heights and made the task of the Excise officers something of a nightmare.

In the face of such taxes many magistrates were very lenient towards smuggling and others were themselves involved in various aspects of the illicit

An illicit still in the Highlands, c. 1800. Two look-outs sound the alert as a party of Excisemen approaches

trade. A classic instance of this was Mr. William Murray the magistrate of Tain, who was also banker and merchant. As the smugglers bought their barley and other goods from him they were seldom convicted in his court. In any event most magistrates were ready to accept a present of whisky, even knowing it to be illicit. The story of a Campbeltown magistrate was typical, when he found himself confounded by the remark of a woman brought before him for distilling illicit whisky. Her defence was: 'I haven'a made a drap since yon wee keg I sent you last week'.

Many of the Excise officers were also guilty of conniving with smugglers and some made considerable fortunes in this way. By giving due warning of when a raid was to be made, or by accepting payment for each keg of spirits passed, they could soon earn a great deal more than their rather poor salaries. At least one Excise officer on his retirement to the south is alleged to have bought himself not just a house, but a whole streetful of houses.

A notable exception was Malcolm Gillespie, who joined the Excise in 1799, aged twenty. Stationed from 1801 to 1807 at Collieston on the Buchan coast above Aberdeen, he seized no less than 10,000 gallons of foreign spirits and destroyed a further 1,000 gallons which he was unable to secure. Scarcely surprisingly, smuggling had all but ceased there by the time he left. From 1807 to 1812 he was stationed at Stonehaven and here after a desperate battle on one occasion he seized a cart and horses with a load of contraband kegs from a notorious smuggler named Grant, who had claimed that the kegs belonged to a local J.P. named Innes.

Two days later when the case came up before the court, Gillespie was disgusted to find that the only magistrate present was Mr. Innes. He 'condemned the spirits, but restored the horse and cart and found the Excise liable in expenses'. Gillespie promptly appealed and was upheld, particularly in view of the fact that the case had been improperly heard in front of only one J.P. On appeal to the Court of Exchequer, Grant was fined £150 and Innes reprimanded, but it is clear that the Excise officers had a hard time of it in circumstances such as these, with little support from anyone.

During a visit to Scotland in 1812, that notable English sportsman, Colonel Peter Hawker, chronicled in his diaries after climbing Ben Lomond:

19th Nov. . . . In several of the most solitary glens we saw the caves where the smugglers manufacture the famous Highland whisky, which is so far superior to the ordinary, by being distilled from the pure malt and smoked with the peat. They usually do this work in the dead of night. . . .

About this period illicit distilling was common near Glasgow. In her *Auto-biography* Mrs. Fletcher, the English wife of an Edinburgh lawyer, mentioned the scene at Balfron in Stirlingshire, where she and her family spent the summer months during the years 1813–1817. She wrote:

Balfron was a most lawless village. . . . It was illicit distillation that demoralised the district. The men of the place resorted to the woods or the sequestered glens among the Campsie Hills, and there distilled whisky, which their wives and daughters took in tin vessels in the form of stays buckled round their waists to sell for a high price in Glasgow.

By 1814 the government in desperation abolished the licence system based on the still capacity and instituted a flat rate of £10. At the same time it re-introduced a system of duty on wash and added a clause prohibiting all stills within the Highland Line under 500 gallons capacity. In the same year, as a result of an action brought by Lowland distillers against the Excise, Highland distillers were forbidden to sell their whisky south of the Highland Line. General Stewart of Garth's view of this was:

It is evident that this law was a complete interdict, as a still of this magnitude would consume more than the disposable grain in the most extensive county within this newly drawn boundary; nor could fuel be obtained for such an establishment without an expense which the community could not possibly bear. The sale, too, of the spirits produced was circumscribed within the same line, and thus the market which alone could have supported the manufacture was entirely cut off. Although the quantity of grain raised within many districts, in consequence of the recent agricultural improvements, greatly exceeds the consumption, the inferior quality of this grain, and the great expense of carrying it to the Lowland distillers, who, by a ready market, and the command of fuel, can more easily accommodate themselves to this law, renders it impracticable for the farmers to dispose of their grain in any manner adequate to pay rents equal to the real value of their farms, subject as they are to the many drawbacks of uncertain climate, uneven surface, distance from market, and scarcity of fuel. Thus hardly any alternative remained but that of having recourse to illicit distillation, or resignation of their farms and breach of their engagements with their landlords. . . . Hence they resort to smuggling as their only resource. If it indeed be true that this illegal traffic has made such deplorable breaches in the honesty and morals of the people, the revenue drawn from the large distilleries, to which the Highlanders have been made the sacrifice, has been procured at too high a price for the country.

According to Ian MacDonald's *Smuggling in the Highlands* no disgrace whatever was attached to being imprisoned for illicit distilling. The prisoners in

Dingwall gaol were treated in the mildest possible way and even allowed out of gaol on Sundays or on special occasions 'and honourably returned'. The height of absurdity seems to have been reached when one prisoner approached the governor with the remarkable proposition that they should set up a still in the prison together.

6. Elizabeth Grant's Memoirs 1812 to Gillespie's Death 1827

'Phairson had a son
Who married Noah's daughter,
And nearly spoiled the flood
By drinking up ta water.
Which he could haf done –
I, at least, pelieve it –
Had ta mixture peen
Only half Glenlivet!

The Massacre of Macpherson,
WILLIAM AYTOUN 1813–1865

It should not be thought that the heavy drinking of the 18th and early 19th centuries was restricted to the men, either in the Highlands or the Lowlands. Alexander Carlyle in his *Autobiography* recalled his boyhood days about 1727 when he toured the Borders with his father and the Rev. Robert Jardine, the

Lochmaben minister. They visited Bridekirk to call on the laird and in his absence were greeted by Lady Bridekirk. Carlyle recorded:

I had never seen such a virago as Lady Bridekirk, not even among the oyster women of Prestonpans. She was like a sergeant of foot in women's clothes, or rather like an over-grown coachman of a Quaker persuasion. On our peremptory refusal to alight, she darted into the house like a hogshead down a slop, and returned instantly with a pint bottle of brandy, a Scots pint I mean – and a stray beer flask, into which she filled almost a bumper. After a long grace said by Mr. Jardine, for it was the third bottle of brandy we had seen since we left Lochmaben – she emptied it to our healths and made the gentlemen follow her example. . . . This lady was famous, even in the Annandale border, both at the bowl and in battle; she could drink a Scots pint of brandy with ease, and when the men grew obstreporous in their cups, she could either put them out of doors or to bed, whichever she found most convenient.

In her *Memoirs of a Highland Lady* Elizabeth Grant recalled being enter-tained at the age of fifteen in 1812 by a Mrs. Macintosh as follows:

The cheer she offered us was never more than bread and cheese and whisky . . . the whisky was a bad habit, there was certainly too much of it going. At every house it was offered, at every house it must be tasted or offence would be given, so we were taught to believe. I am sure now that had we steadily refused compliance with so incorrect a custom it would have been far better for ourselves, and might all the sooner have put a stop to so pernicious a habit among the people. Whisky-drinking was and is the bane of that country; from early morning till late at night it went on. Decent gentlewomen began the day with a dram. In our house the bottle of whisky, with its accompaniment of a silver salver full of small glasses, was placed on the side-table with cold meat every morning. In the pantry a bottle of whisky was the allowance per day, with bread and cheese in required quantity, for such messengers or visitors whose errands sent them in that direction. The very poorest cottages could offer whisky; all the men engaged in the wood manufacture drank it in goblets three times a day, yet except at a merry-making we never saw any one tipsy.

She went on to refer to the drinking habits of the timber workers on the Spey, whom she visited occasionally in 1813 when aged sixteen:

When the men met in the morning they were supposed to have breakfasted at home, and had perhaps had their private dram, it being cold work in a dark wintry dawn, to start over the moor for a walk of some miles to end standing up to their knees in water; yet on collecting whisky was always handed round; a lad with a small cask – a quarter anker – on his back, and a horn cup in his hand that held a gill, appeared three times a day among them. They all took their 'morning' raw, undiluted and without accompaniment, so they did the gill at parting when the work was done; but the noontide dram was part of a meal. There was a twenty minutes' rest from labour, and a bannock and a bit of cheese taken out of every pocket to be eaten leisurely with the whisky. When we were there the horn cup was offered first to us, and each of us took a cup to the health of our friends around us, who all stood up. Sometimes a floater's wife or bairn would come with a message; such messenger was always offered whisky. Aunt Mary had a story that one day a woman with a child in her arms, and another bit thing at her knee, came up among them; the horn cup was duly handed to her, she took a 'gey guid drap' herself, and then gave a little to each of the babies. 'My goodness, child', said my mother to the wee thing that was trotting by the mother's side, 'doesn't it *bite* you?' 'Ay, but I like the bite', replied the creature.

Despite the 1814 Act, or perhaps largely because of it, illicit distilling and smuggling were never so prevalent in the Highlands, or in Scotland as a whole, as they were during the second decade of the 19th century. By the time of Waterloo, in 1815, the illicit distillers were in full swing throughout the country despite the efforts of the Excise officers. Amongst the more notorious and thriving centres of illicit distilling in the Highlands was the Glenlivet area, by this time reputed to have as many as two hundred illicit stills.

Prominent amongst the Glenlivet farmers and distillers – for the two generally went together – was Andrew Smith, born in 1742, the son of John Gow, alias Smith, and father of George Smith, by this time a qualified architect and builder. Although at this stage in his seventies, Andrew Smith was known as a fine farmer and distiller, producing a hogshead a week of illicit whisky by the time of Waterloo. On his death in 1817 his son George, a strong, upstanding, bold young man of twenty-five, gave up his career as an architect and builder and took over the farm of Upper Drumin. In a short while he was recognised as one of the more daring and successful illicit distillers in the glen.

It was perhaps fortunate for them both that George Smith and Malcolm Gillespie, the hard-working and ill-rewarded Excise officer, by this time stationed back in Aberdeenshire, never came into direct contact with each other. Gillespie's frequent severe clashes with smugglers provide an insight into the hard life endured by the honest Excise officer, who was grossly underpaid and expected to eke out his living on the seizures he made. Although this might sound like a reasonable incentive in theory, when it came to the point he was expected to share the proceeds equally with the Treasury as well as paying all the solicitors' fees and other expenses connected with each seizure. In practice it was a thankless way to earn a living and it is understandable why so few Excise officers at this time were above accepting a bribe from smugglers.

Perhaps typical of the fierce engagements Gillespie had with smuggling gangs was one on the night of December 30th 1818, near Kintore in Aberdeenshire. Here he encountered a dozen or so Highlanders with five horses and 160 gallons of illicit whisky. In a free fight with the gang he was knocked to the ground by weight of numbers and hacked with his own sabre wrenched from his hand, but drawing his pistol he fired two shots and wounded the leader in the shoulder and thigh. Sinking his teeth into the thumb of another smuggler who was doing his best to throttle him, Gillespie managed to regain his feet. Finally, with the aid of his assistants, all firing together, the gang was driven off into the hills. Sending his assistants after them, Gillespie stayed with the contraband, no doubt feeling justifiably pleased with himself, but bleeding from several wounds and obviously badly shaken by the beating he had received.

A first-hand account of the behaviour of the Highland smugglers is given by the Rev. Thomas Guthrie, who recalled seeing them often in his boyhood around this period, 1818. He recorded:

When a boy in Brechin, I was quite familiar with the appearance and on-goings of the Highland smugglers. They rode on Highland ponies, carrying on each side of their small, shaggy, but brave and hardy steeds, a small cask, or 'keg', as it was called, of illicit whisky manufactured amid the wilds of Aberdeenshire, or the glens of the Grampians. They took up a position on some commanding eminence during the day, where they could, as from a watch tower, descry the distant approach of the enemy, the exciseman or gauger; then, when night fell, every man to horse, descending the mountains only six miles from Brechin, they scoured the plains, rattled into the villages and towns, disposing of their whisky to agents they had everywhere; and, now safe, returned at their leisure, or often in a triumphal procession. . . . I have seen a troop of thirty of them riding in Indian file, and in broad day, through the streets of Brechin, after they had succeeded in disposing of their whisky, and, as they rode leisurely along, beating time with their formidable cudgels on the empty barrels to the great amusement of the public and mortification of the excisemen. . . . Everybody, with few exceptions drank what was in reality illicit whisky – far superior to that made under the eye of the Excise – lords and lairds, members of Parliament and ministers of the gospel and everybody else.

The same sort of scene was commonplace throughout the Highlands and an eye-witness description from the other side of Scotland is provided by Joseph Mitchell, Chief Superintendent of the Highland Roads, who encountered a smuggling gang around 1820 and recorded the event in his *Reminiscences* as follows:

One morning as I was driving up Glenmoriston before breakfast, and taking a turn in the road of that beautiful valley, I saw before me at some little distance about twenty-five Highland horses tied to each other, and carrying two kegs of whisky each. They were attended by ten or twelve men, some in kilts and all with bonnets and plaids, and carrying large bludgeons. When they saw me approach two of them fell back until I came up with them. They scrutinised me sharply and said: 'It is a fine morning, sir;' to which I responded. Then one turned to the other and said, 'Ha rickh shealass ha mach Mitchell fere rate – mohr;' the literal translation of which is, 'you need not mind; it is the son of Mitchell, the man of the high roads.'

He then turned to me and said, 'Would you took a dram?' and on my assenting he took out of his pocket a round tin snuff box, then common, but without the lid, holding about a large wine-glassful, and filled it with whisky from a bottle which he took from his side pocket.

After some kindly greeting and talk and drinking my dram, I passed on, the other men politely touching their bonnets as I left.

John Mackenzie, uncle of Osgood Mackenzie of Gairloch, is quoted in the latter's *Hundred Years in the Highlands* as saying of the period around the second decade of the century:

Even so late as then, say 1820, one would go a long way before one met a person who shrank from smuggling. My father never tasted any but smuggled whisky, and when every mortal that called for him – they were legion daily – had a dram instantly poured into him, the ankers of whisky emptied yearly must have been numerous indeed. I don't believe my mother or he ever dreamed that smuggling was a crime. Ere I was twenty he had paid £1,000 . . . to make me a commissioner of supply and consequently a Justice of the Peace . . . and before it had occurred to me that smuggling was really a serious breach of the law, I had from the bench fined many a poor smuggler as the law directs. Then I began to see that the 'receiver' – myself, for instance, as I drank only 'mountain dew' then – was worse than the smuggler. So ended all my connection with smuggling except in my capacity as magistrate, to the grief of at least one of my old friends and visitors, the Dean of Ross and Argyle, who scoffed at my resolution and looked sorrowfully back on the happy times when he was young and his father distilled every Saturday what was needed for the following week.

Joseph Mitchell in his *Reminiscences* confirmed this, stating categorically: 'Almost all wines, spirits and foreign commodities to the Highlands were smuggled. . . .' Yet the Rev. Thomas Guthrie, Joseph Mitchell and John Mackenzie were all writing as old men reminiscing about their youth. They could not look back on the half-century previous to 1800 and make comparisons as General David Stewart of Garth could and did in his *Sketches of the Character, Manners and Present State of the Highlanders of Scotland*, written in 1822 with a lifetime of experience at first hand. He emphasised the steady growth of smuggling in the previous century from the 1770s, following repressive laws after the rebellion of 1745 and subsequent ill-judged legislation. He wrote:

So little was it practiced in the Perthshire Highlands that a tenant of my grandfather's was distinguished by the appellation of 'Donald Whisky', from his being a distiller and smuggler of that spirit. If all existing were to be named from this traffic, five of the most numerous clans of the country conjoined could not produce so many of one name. In the year 1778, there was only one officer of Excise in that part of Perthshire above Dunkeld, and he had little employment. In the same district there are now eleven resident officers in full activity, besides Rangers (as they are called) and extra officers sent to see that the resident officers are doing their duty; yet so rapidly did illicit distillation increase, that it would seem as if the greater the number of officers appointed, the more employment they found for themselves; and it is a common, and I believe, a just remark, that whenever an officer is placed in a glen, he is not long without business. . . .

General Stewart's comments on this early application of Parkinson's Law – that Excise officers increased to fill the glens available – obviously had some grounds for justification. Certainly by 1822, as the Rev. Thomas Guthrie indicated, everyone drank illicit whisky, 'lords, lairds, members of Parliament' and even eventually the King himself: for when George IV visited Scotland in that year he was provided, by his own request, with illicit whisky.

In his biography of Sir Walter Scott, J. G. Lockhart described the arrival of the royal yacht at Leith in pouring rain on the 14th of August, 1822:

. . . Sir Walter rowed off to the Royal George, and, says the newspaper of the day, 'To this record let me add, that, on receiving the Poet on the quarter-deck, his Majesty called for a bottle of Highland whisky, and having drunk his health in this national liquor, desired a glass to be filled for him . . .'

By this time a corpulent, corsetted and creaking figure, George IV's visit was largely stage-managed by the 'wizard of the north' who as well as being a best-selling author was no mean showman. Insisting on dressing in full Highland regalia, superintended by none other than General Sir David Stewart of Garth, it is reported that the king also insisted on wearing flesh-coloured tights beneath his kilt to preserve the decencies.

The occasion and the source of the royal whisky is well described by Elizabeth Grant:

The whole country went mad. Everybody stormed every point to get to Edinburgh to receive him. Sir Walter Scott and the Town Council were overwhelming themselves with preparations . . . the King wore at the Levee the Highland dress. . . . Someone objecting to this dress, particularly on so large a man, 'Nay' said she [Lady Saltoun, noted for her wit] 'we should take it very kind of him; since his stay will be so short, the more we see of him the better'. Sir William Curtis [the Lord Mayor of London] was kilted too, and standing near the King, many persons mistook them, amongst others John Hamilton Dundas, who kneeled to kiss the fat Alderman's hand, when, finding out his mistake, he called out 'Wrong, by Jove!' and rising, moved on undaunted to the larger presence. One incident connected with this time made me very cross. Lord Conynghame, the Chamberlain, was looking everywhere for the pure Glenlivet whisky; the King drank nothing else. It was not to be had out of the Highlands. My father sent word to me – I was the cellarer – to empty my pet bin, where was whisky long in the wood, long in uncorked bottles, mild as milk, and the true contraband gout to it. . . . The whisky and fifty brace of ptarmigan all shot by one man went up to Holyrood House and were graciously received and made much of. . . .

It made nonsense of Acts of Parliament when M.P.s like Sir Peter Grant, Elizabeth Grant's father, bought only illicit whisky from Glenlivet, distilled by George Smith at Upper Drumin, or his neighbours. When it could also be said that the King himself drank 'nothing else', the situation was well past the point of absurdity. Yet this was the result of endless Acts of Parliament since the Union in 1707. Small wonder that the legislators were baffled by the situation and unable to decide what action to take for the best.

By this time the Excise was using an instrument known as a saccharometer, which accurately measured the specific gravity of the wash. It had been known as early as 1798, but the first occasion it was used was by an Act of 1816, which applied only to Scotland. By Acts of 1817 and 1818 the old inaccurate Clarke's hydrometer was superseded by a hydrometer of much more efficient design invented by Bartholomew Sikes, who had been Secretary to the English Board of Excise. Sikes's hydrometer was taken as an accurate measure of proof, now at last defined as that 'which at a temperature of fifty-one degrees Fahrenheit weighs exactly 12/13 of an equal measure of distilled water'. With accompanying tables it was thus possible to work out at once from Sikes's hydrometer the percentage of proof spirit from the reading of the instrument.

Under an Act of 1820 the saccharometer and Sikes's hydrometer were to be used in conjunction. Thus the Excise officer had first to check the wash, then the spirit, for specific gravity and an accurate check could be kept on the whole brewing and distilling process. The objection from the distiller's viewpoint was that he was unable in these circumstances to brew and distil at the same time. The explanation in a report by the Commissioners of Revenue Inquiry of 1823 was:

This regulation enables the Officer to give his separate attention to each successive part of the process of manufacture and renders the concealment of any wash, or use of it, if concealed, extremely difficult; while the access of the distiller to the utensils required for distillation is unnecessary except during the time that the process is going on under the survey of the officer. It is true that this prohibition prevents the manufacturers from mixing the residuum from the wash still with that of the mash tun, by which, it is said, both are made fitter for the use of cattle and he may in consequence experience some loss. We cannot view this objection however as of sufficient importance to weigh against the indisputable security the regulation affords to the Revenue and we therefore recommend its continuance.

Meanwhile the Duke of Gordon, one of the largest landowners in Scotland, particularly in Inverness-shire and Banffshire, two of the great whisky distilling areas, had spoken out in the House of Lords in 1822 during debates on the future measures to be taken on illicit distilling in the Highlands. He pointed out that whisky was the national and traditional drink of the Highlands, that the High-lander could not be prevented from distilling it and that it was natural for him to wish to do so. He went on to guarantee that, if reasonably realistic legislation was passed providing an opportunity for the legal distilling of whisky of as good quality as that produced by illicit stills, he and the other large landed proprietors would do their utmost to suppress illicit distilling and to encourage their tenants to license their stills.

As a result of the Duke of Gordon's intervention and the report of a commission under Mr. Thomas Wallace (subsequently Lord Wallace) of the Board of Trade, the 1823 Act to Eliminate Illicit Distilling was duly passed. By this Act a flat licence rate of £10 was set for stills of forty gallons capacity upwards, thus setting a minimum size of forty gallons rather than the totally unrealistic five hundred gallons of the 1814 Act. A duty of 2s 3d was set for each gallon of proof spirit distilled.

The first to take out a licence under the new Act was George Smith, erstwhile architect and builder, now farmer and illicit distiller on the farm of Upper Drumin in Glenlivet. Shrewder and more far-sighted than his fellows, he realised that the new Act had made the distilling of legal whisky a feasible proposition. He also saw that illicit distilling could not go on for ever. Furthermore he received considerable encouragement, as he was the first to admit, from his landlord, the Duke of Gordon, who was naturally keen to make good his bold assurance to the House of Lords. With his backing George Smith built himself a new distillery on his farm at Upper Drumin.

This distillery built at Upper Drumin in Glenlivet was in many ways typical of others to follow in the Highlands. It was on the site of an old illicit distillery, with pure water from the Livet and inexhaustible springs nearby, as well as the finest peat from the Faemussach peatfield close to hand. Barley was obtained from the Laich of Moray and the farms nearby. Its only disadvantage was its remoteness, necessitating lengthy transport by pack horses thirty-five miles to the coast once the whisky was distilled. Initially the remoteness had other disadvantages, for George Smith's erstwhile smuggling comrades soon threatened him with dire consequences. He later described the events that followed thus:

When the new Act was heard of in Glenlivet and in the Highlands of Aberdeenshire, they ridiculed the idea that anyone should be found daring enough to start legal distilling in their midst. The proprietors were very anxious to fulfil their pledge to the Government and did everything they could to encourage the commencement of legal distilling; but the desperate character of the smugglers and the violence of their threats deterred anyone for some time. At length in 1824, I, George Smith, who was then a robust young fellow, and not given to be easily 'fleggit', determined to chance it. I was already a tenant of the Duke and received every encouragement from his Grace and his factor Mr. Skinner. The outlook was an ugly one, though. I was warned by my civil neighbours that they meant to burn the new distillery to the ground and me in the heart of it. The laird of Aberlour had presented me with a pair of hair trigger pistols worth ten guineas, and they were never out of my belt for years. I got together two or three stout fellows for servants, armed them with pistols and let it be known everywhere that I would fight for my place to the last shot. I had a good character as a man of my word and, through watching by turns every night for years, we contrived to save the distillery from the fate so freely predicted for it. But I often, both at kirk and market had rough times of it among the glen people. . . .

The 'pair of hair trigger pistols' were only discharged on one occasion. George Smith was returning from a successful journey south after selling his whisky when he stopped at the inn at Cock Bridge, a wild and desolate spot in the hills. His money belt was well filled with gold sovereigns and he noticed some of the more ruffianly company there thoughtfully eyeing its bulk around his middle as he warmed himself before the heavily banked peat fire. Overhearing one of them muttering to another that they might take the chance of lifting the gold they knew it must contain, he did not wait for them to start an unequal contest. Cocking one of his pistols he fired it straight into the base of the pile of peats raising a 'stour' of white ash which obscured everything from view and filled the eyes of all the company. When they had recovered themselves with a good deal of cursing it was only to discover that George Smith had taken advantage of the confusion to slip out to his horse and make good his escape.

He was not a man to be easily deterred, but he recorded:

In 1825 and 1826 three more legal distilleries were commenced in the glen, but the smugglers soon succeeded in frightening away their occupants, none of whom ventured to hang on a single year in the face of the threats uttered so freely against them. Threats were not the only weapons used. In 1825 a distillery which had just been started near the Banks o' Dee at the head of Aberdeenshire was burnt to the ground with all its outbuildings and the distiller had a narrow escape from being roasted in his own kiln. The country was in a very lawless state at the time. The riding officers of the Revenue were the mere sport of smugglers and nothing was more common than for them to be shown a still at work and then coolly defied to make a seizure.

This was no exaggeration, as Malcolm Gillespie could bear witness. In 1824 he confronted a gang of 'from 25 to 30 men' with horses and carts full of whisky which they were taking to Aberdeen. They contemptuously refused to stop, so he shot the leading horse and, on being attacked by their leader with a large bludgeon, he shot him in the shoulder. In his own words: 'a terrible conflict ensued. Bloody heads, hats rolling in the roads, the reports of alternate firing and other noise, resembled more the battle of Waterloo than the interception of a band of lawless desperadoes – but in the end they were obliged to lay down their arms. . . . It was fortunate no lives were lost on this memorable occasion'. The seizure consisted of 14 horses and 10 carts, with 410 gallons of whisky and 80 gallons destroyed. Gillespie and his assistants were severely wounded and bruised, but the smugglers were in an even worse state.

It is likely that some of George Smith's neighbours were involved in that desperate affray with Malcolm Gillespie and this could well have influenced his decision to take out a licence to distil legally in 1824. A letter from Malcolm Gillespie regarding the sale of the 'very best Glenlivet' whisky, the proceeds of the seizure, remains extant, addressed to Thomas Syme, Esq., W.S., Edinburgh.

Crombie Cottage, Skene, by Aberdeen, 9th February, 1824.
Sir, I received yours of the 5th current in due course and beg to acquaint you in answer as you desire that you will very probably see by the Public Printers that I have within 8 days made one of the most extensive seizures ever captured in the north of Scotland of the very best *Glenlivet*.

With regard to the prices, they are uncertain to a few shillings as the smugglers themselves have been getting from £5.15 to £6 per anker of 10 Gallons this some time back without Permit and to be candid with you the fact is that the new Distilling Laws and the indulgence to Legal Distillation has in a very trifling degree reduced whisky in this quarter as our North Country Gentry will not drink the Large Still Whisky.

As the sale of my whisky will take place in a few days I shall be glad to have as many orders from you and your friends as you can procure, as I can with confidence recommend this article as of the very best as to strength and flavour and the names and addresses of those friends will require to be particularised so that regular Permits may be issued and proper tickets affixed to their respective quantities. At the same time you will be pleased to say on whom I am to draw for the amount. I am, Sir, M. Gillespie.

By the end of 1824, after twenty-five years' service, Gillespie was obviously beginning to feel the strain of this kind of encounter. In a rather pathetic twenty-nine page statement, or 'Memorial', to his superior officers in the Excise he detailed his successes and the many wounds and injuries he had suffered over the years. After listing his seizures he ended by pointing out that, far from earning him a fortune, they had cost him about £1 an anker (i.e. ten gallons) due to the expenses he had incurred in paying informants and having to keep three or four assistants 'at board, bed and lodging and pay . . . all of which *comes out of the Memorialist's own pocket*'. He ended by submitting 'that he humbly considers himself entitled to some remuneration and beneficial appointment suited to his time of life and bodily infirmity'.

It is a lasting reflection on his superior officers that they appear to have ignored his appeal for help. Gillespie was an Excise officer of rare character and initiative and had thoroughly earned promotion to a less arduous post. Among other innovations he trained a dog to seize the smugglers' horses and had great success with it, before it was shot one day in a skirmish with smugglers, much to his grief. During his service he was wounded in no less than forty-two parts of his body. His total seizures were over 85 carts, 166 horses, 407 stills, 6,535 gallons of whisky, 14,000 gallons of foreign spirit and 62,400 gallons of wash. In the end, his appeal ignored, finding himself in debt, he foolishly forged some Treasury Bills. In 1827 he was arrested, tried and found guilty. Despite signed attestations by many influential people as to the value of his twenty-eight years' service, he was hanged two months later. He deserved a better end.

VI *The Porteous Mob* [1736] by James Drummond (1816–1877)

VII *Highland Hospitality* by John Frederick Lewis (1805–1876)

VIII *The Scottish Whisky Still* (1819) by Sir David Wilkie (1785–1841)

IX *The Illicit Still* by Sir Edwin Landseer (1802–1873)

Opposite:

X, XI Tradition and change. While tasting calls for the same critical eye and nose as in Wilkie's day, the modern distillery control panel is a far cry from Landseer's scene

XII Glenlivet and its distillery

7. Effects of 1823 Act to Outbreak of Crimean War 1854

Inspiring bold *John Barleycorn*!
What dangers thou canst make us scorn!
Wi' tippeny, we fear nae evil:
Wi' usquabae, we'll face the devil!

Tam o' Shanter, ROBERT BURNS 1791

The efforts of alert and vigilant Excisemen such as Gillespie were still required long after the 1823 Act, for this was no immediate panacea, as George Smith's struggles testify. Yet before the 1823 reforms in Excise the total tax-paid whisky consumed had sunk as low as two million gallons. By 1825 the figure had risen to very nearly six million gallons. A further 'Consolidation Act' in 1825 made the regulations regarding the manufacture of spirits uniform in England, Scotland and Ireland, except for a few minor details and, of course, the duty payable, which remained different in each country.

The immediate increase in sales caused legal distillers to welcome the provisions of the 1823 Act. A distiller in the Crieff area of Perthshire, Mr. Andrew Bannerman, is on record as stating (during a Parliamentary Commission sitting from 1833–36):

In forty years experience of the distillery, I never knew a law made by the Legislature that was so complete, either for securing the revenue, or improving the quality of spirits, or suppressing illicit distillation. . . . The law has answered our most sanguine expectations, that of the Government, and that of the legal distiller; and it affords an encouragement to the agriculturalist for the distilleries are now generally diffused all over Scotland.

The very success of the measures, however, proved too great a temptation for the Exchequer. The tax per Imperial gallon, the universally recognised measure under the Consolidation Act, was only 2s 4d in 1825. In 1826 it was raised to 2s 10d and in 1830 to 3s 4d. The immediate effect was the encouragement of illicit distilling and a fall in the consumption of legal spirit once more.

Another source of trouble was a measure referred to as a drawback, or rebate, on malt, amounting to 1s 2d per gallon, allowing two gallons per bushel. This was introduced in an attempt to encourage the small distiller, particularly in the Highlands, to enter the trade legally. It was intended to provide him with the opportunity to distil malt whisky at the same rate of duty as the grain distillers, but the Lowland grain distillers, unable to claim this rebate, naturally objected to it.

The favourable effects of this rebate are made clear in a résumé by Captain H. Munro, who owned the Teaninich distillery in Ross-shire (made to the Parliamentary Commission 1833–36):

Since 1795 I have resided in this county, engaged in farming . . . until 1817 . . . all the . . . farmers . . . were in the habit of openly disposing of the barley raised on their farms to the smugglers, for there were only one or two small distilleries in this county. . . . In the year 1817 the . . . Commissioners of Supply of Ross . . . did . . . encourage the erection of distilleries . . . accordingly, three or four were built . . . the Teaninich distillery was built by me on my own property; yet it so happened that the illicit distillers commanded the grain market of the country . . . smuggling still existed, and the success of the distilleries disappointed the expectations of those who carried them on . . . but I continued to struggle on; and when the favourable Distillery Laws took place in 1823, with the drawback of 1s 2d per gallon on malt, to the extent of two shillings per bushel, an extraordinary change was soon perceived; smuggling was greatly suppressed, and for one gallon . . . from my distillery previous to 1823, there were, from that time till 1830, an increase of from thirty to forty times the quantity . . . consumed. . . .

Whether legally or illegally distilled, the fame of Glenlivet whisky continued to be spread abroad. In 1827 in the *Noctes Ambrosianae*, the famous series of sketches in *Blackwood's Magazine* by John Wilson, Professor of Moral Philosophy at Edinburgh University under his pen name of Christopher North, there appeared the following dialogue attributed to the Ettrick Shepherd, based on James Hogg:

Shepherd: Gie's your haun again, my dear sir. Noo, what shall we hae?

North: A single jug, James, of Glenlivet – not very strong if you please; for ——

Shepherd: A single jug o' Glenlivet no very strang! My dear sir, hae you lost your judgement? You ken my recate for toddy, and ye never saw's fail yet. In wi' a' the sugar, and a' the whusky, whatever they chance to be, intil the jug about half fu' o' water – just say three minutes to get aff the boil – and then the King's health in a bumper.

In a further sketch Christopher North quoted James Hogg once again eulogising malt whisky in the shape of Glenlivet as follows:

Gie me the real Glenlivet, and I weel believe I could mak' drinking toddy oot o' sea-water. The human mind never tires o' Glenlivet, any mair than o' caller air. If a body could just find oot the exac' proportion and quantity that ought to be drunk every day, and keep to that, I verily trow that he might leeve for ever, without dying at a', and that doctors and kirkyards would go oot o' fashion.

The year 1828, however, saw a revolutionary development in whisky distilling. Robert Stein, a member of the prominent whisky distilling family, invented and tried out a new form of continuous still, so-called because it distilled in one process without the double distillation required by pot stills. Despite the fact that it was a complicated process involving heated wash being sprayed into a cylinder where it was stripped of its alcohol by steam, the verdict of the Excise officers attending its inception and trial was that 'the spirits . . . are much more pure and wholesome than those produced by common distillation'.

By the time William IV had succeeded to the throne on the death of George IV in 1830 a Stein still had been built at their distillery in Kirkliston and another at the Haig distillery at Cameron Bridge, for the Steins and Haigs were now related by marriage. In 1831, however, Aeneas Coffey, the ex-Inspector General of Excise in Ireland, invented another type of continuous still. For this he was granted a fourteen-year patent in 1832 and a prototype was set up in the Dock

Distillery, Dublin. The new still, which soon proved itself more efficient than the Stein invention, was alternatively known either as the Coffey still or the patent still. Whisky distilled from it was known as patent-still whisky, or grain whisky, as opposed to malt whisky distilled from malt in the time-honoured way through two pot stills.

The patent-still whisky is made primarily from grain – from oats, rye, or maize if available – with the addition of a little malt in the fermenting process. The grain is first crushed and then pressure boiled to break up the starch. A small proportion of malt is then added during the mashing to enhance the required saccharifying process. Fermentation is on a much larger scale than for pot stills since the amount put through a patent still is many times greater. The wash is pumped in at one end and comes out as alcohol at the other in a continuous flow.

In essence the patent still consists of two larger copper columns about forty feet high side by side and linked by a junction pipe at the top. The columns are termed the analyser and rectifier. Each is divided into a series of horizontal perforated chambers. The wash is pumped in through a coiled pipe running down the length of the rectifier ingeniously serving as a coolant for that side as well as a means of heating the wash before it enters the top of the analyser. Here it encounters an upwards pressure of steam coming through the perforated chambers. Since alcohol boils and evaporates at a lower temperature than water, as the wash slowly descends, chamber by chamber, the alcohol is separated from it and rises with the steam, being then directed into the base of the rectifier column. The steam then condenses on the cooling plates of the rectifier chamber by chamber. The purest alcohol rises to the top, but the heavier higher alcohols and lower alcohols condense earlier, since they have a lower boiling point, and are drawn off to be re-distilled. The final product of the rectifier is almost pure alcohol.

The process of operation of the patent still is continuous and can go on for as long as the wash is flowing. In a matter of hours thousands of gallons can be produced and there is no comparison for speed with the older and much slower methods of producing malt whisky by two separate distillations in two different pot stills. The grain whisky is also a much purer spirit, in that it lacks the same degree of higher alcohols and similar impurities which add flavour and taste to the malt whisky.

This did not meet with universal approval by any means. As early as 1831 a Major Cumming Bruce was fulminating in a letter to the *Inverness Courier:*

It is asserted that the rage for the use of whisky is still increasing, while to our sad experience we know that its quality is deteriorating among us. It is no longer the pure dew of the mountain which issued from the bothies of our free traders of the hills, healthful and as exhilerating as the drops which the sun's first rays drink up from the heathbell of the Cairngorms, but a vile, rascally, mixed compotation which fires the blood and maddens the veins without warming the heart, or, like the old, elevating the understanding.

If, as one assumes, Major Cumming Bruce had been drinking grain whisky and comparing it with malt whisky, his diatribe is perfectly understandable. For a start, as already indicated, the ingredients are not the same. Apart from a small proportion of barley malt used in the mash to turn the starch more readily into sugar, the grains used are generally rye, oats, or maize when available. The resulting spirit is much lighter than malt whisky and without the same distinctive flavours, although it would be incorrect to term it pure alcohol, since traces of the higher, or lower, alcohols, which in part give malt whisky its distinctive flavour, are also present, though to a much lesser degree, in grain whisky. There are not, and cannot be, the peaty flavours, or aromatic taste, which distinguish a good malt whisky.

Surprisingly enough, although the Coffey still was patented and approved in 1832, the Excise officers did not receive instructions on overseeing the working of these stills from the Board of Excise until 1838. Since the production costs of grain whisky in a patent still were considerably lower than the production costs of malt whisky in a pot still, there seems to have been something of a rush to set up patent-still distilleries, although few of them survived.

A number of varied factors, the increased duty per gallon, the reduction of 6d on the malt drawback, the increase in cheap grain whisky production with the development of the patent stills, more distillers climbing onto the bandwagon of apparent prosperity, dissension between Highland malt and Lowland grain distillers, or more simply a recurrence of the old rivalry between Highlander and Lowlander, all combined to have a drastic effect on the whisky-distilling industry. The figures for the consumption of duty-paid whisky speak for themselves. In 1830 they were six million gallons. In 1831 a decrease was already noticeable. By 1834 they were less than one and a quarter million gallons, even less than before the 1823 Act.

There was naturally considerable alarm at these figures, for everyone was agreed that the amount of whisky drunk had not decreased. There was a wide-spread resurgence of illicit distilling, as well as significant evasion by some of the distillers themselves. By tightening their controls the Excise managed to bring the problem under control, even though it involved bringing a Revenue cruiser back on patrol to ensure that no whisky was run by sea across the border into England.

The Parliamentary Commission under Sir Henry Parnell which was appointed to investigate the liquor trade and which sat from 1833 to 1836, uncovered some interesting information, but in the nature of things proved largely ineffectual. They were surprised to find that the 1823 reforms had been on the whole extremely successful. Their conclusions were basically that malt whisky was important to Scotland because it was the national drink and if the licensed distillers were not encouraged it would be illegally distilled. They stated it long-windedly thus:

Whatever relates to the manufacture and regulation of malt spirits must be considered as a subject of peculiar interest with regard to Scotland, because this description of spirit has long been established by the prevailing taste as the national beverage of that part of the kingdom, and because there can be no doubt that, for the supply of a demand so universal, there will always be found within the country the means of a corresponding extent of production; it follows, that unless these means are provided under sanction of the law, they will be furnished from private and unauthorised sources, and therefore it becomes peculiarly important, with respect to Scotland, that such encouragement should be given to the licenced distiller.

The Commission discovered good reasons for the antagonism between the Highland malt distillers and the Lowland grain distillers. The latter were in the habit of setting up one of their staff as a dealer in spirits close to the distillery. He would then be allowed to mix grain and malt spirits in large quantities, which were shipped to the Highland areas to be sold as malt spirits at a much lower price than the Highland malts. Furthermore the Lowland grain distillers wanted the malt drawback withdrawn and the Highland malt distillers depended on this for their existence.

Mr. Robert M'Laren of John Bald and Company at Carsebridge revealed another source of bitterness in the laws regarding distilling. By these, originally, a distiller was entitled to change from working grain to working malt after a full month's working and six days' notice of his intention to change. Then the law was altered and no change was permitted within a licence year. The result was that people with sufficient capital to own two distilleries were at a great advantage. The output of one would be used to undercut a competitor by swamping the market, while raising the price of the other known to be in short supply.

M'Laren also revealed that the prohibition under the Act against grain and malt distilleries, or the brewery and rectifying plant, being within a quarter mile of one another was often broken. He described a distillery of this kind:

The shaft of the steam engine serves for both the malt and grain distillery.

They may transfer malt to the grain distillery and so evade malt duty.

The Excise has no check on what they put into the grain spirits.

They turn one large work into two by putting up a partition with the same machine grinding grain and bruising malt.

Clearly the Excise officials were often failing to do their job efficiently. Furthermore certain of the restrictions which were imposed tended to affect sales adversely. For example, it was forbidden to export spirits in casks under eighty gallons in size. The Commission went so far as to quote favourably the suggestion of a senior Excise officer 'that an arrangement might be made under which the exportation of Scotch spirits in bottles might be permitted in the same way as is practised with respect to foreign wines'.

The Commission probably did some good, if only by exposing some of the more flagrant abuses as well as some of the absurdities of the 1823 Act. Furthermore, by noting publicly the inadequacies of the Excise in certain respects, they encouraged the Board to take stronger action. Throughout the 1830s and 1840s, however, there continued to be considerable friction between the Highland malt distillers and the Lowland grain distillers. The grain whisky chiefly found a market in the large Lowland towns and in England, where it was generally turned into gin. The malt whisky continued to find a market principally in the Highlands and the north-east Lowlands, as well as among the more discerning in the southern and central Lowlands. A direct trade with the U.S.A., however, was started as early as 1824 when 1,500 gallons were sent from Islay. By 1834 the figure had risen to 25,000 gallons.

The 1830s saw one development outside the whisky-distilling industry which was to have a considerable effect on both grain and malt whisky distillers. In 1832 at Preston in Lancashire the Temperance Movement first adopted the principle of total abstinence. The Rev. Robert Gray Mason came to Scotland in the 1830s with the half-preaching, half-missionary, wholly earnest ardour of the rabid teetotaller, which had proved so effective in the south. In a short while Total Abstinence Societies had been founded in a number of areas, dedicated to a radical change in the drinking habits of the country. A number of influential figures soon joined them. Among the founder members of the Glasgow Temperance Society was William Collins, later to make his fortune as a publisher of Temperance literature.

It was perhaps significant that the arrival of the young Queen Victoria on the throne in 1837 should be heralded by a strong upsurge of Temperance. The old habits of the previous century were giving way to changing social customs. It is only necessary to look at the figures for the seizures of illicit stills by the Excise officers to be aware of the change. In 1823 there had been 1,400 seizures of stills, but by 1834 the figure had been reduced to 692. There was no doubt that illicit distilling was on the wane at last.

Perhaps even more significant was the number of new distilleries which were founded in much the same period. In 1830 the Talisker distillery was started on the Isle of Skye. In 1832 the Glen Scotia distillery was founded in Campbeltown by Stewart Galbraith. In 1836 Robert Hay founded the Glenfarclas distillery not far from Glenlivet. In 1840 the brothers James and John Grant, who came from an old farming family in the Laich of Moray and therefore by inference knew a good deal about distilling already, started a large new distillery in Rothes known as the Glen Grant distillery. The elder brother James was trained as a banker and lawyer and the younger was a farmer with a keen business mind, so that the distillery flourished from the earliest days. In the same year a farmer, James Gray, in East Lothian started a Lowland malt distillery at Glenkinchie. Then in 1842 in Tain, Ross-shire, much further north, the Glenmorangie distillery was founded by William Mathieson. Thus throughout Scotland there was a significant upsurge in whisky distilling. It was gradually ceasing to be a predominantly illegal cottage industry and growing to be a national industry of importance.

Yet old habits die hard and there were still some smugglers who clearly enjoyed pitting their wits against the Excisemen. Alfred Barnard in his book *The Whisky Distilleries of the United Kingdom*, published in 1887, recounts the story of a notable smuggler named Stewart in the Strath Tay district about 1845:

The famous Stewart arrived at a place near Perth with a boatload of potheen. He had sent up to the town for assistance to remove the Whisky when . . . the Revenue Officers appeared on the scene. Stewart immediately rowed out to mid-stream, but the officers seeing an idle boat followed him . . . seeing that he was closely pressed and that

14   *The Smugglers' Intrusion* (c. 1824) after Sir David Wilkie (1785–1841)

15, 16   *Landing a Smuggled Cargo by Night* and *The Smugglers' Cove*: two romanticised views of the smuggling trade

17   *The Old Excise Office, Edinburgh* by Walter Geikie (1795–1837)

18   'The deil's awa' wi' th'Exciseman' (Robert Burns, *The Exciseman*)

19   The Glenlivet distillery, 1887

20   George Smith (1792–1871),
founder of the Glenlivet distillery in
1824

Old Gent. (*nervous*). "BAD THING, WHISKEY, FOR SHAVING!"
Barber. "OU AY—ATWEEL IT IS—MAKS THE SKIN UNCO' TENDER; BUT I'LL TAK' GREAT CARE."

THE UNCO' GUID.

Scrupulous Waiter. "A WHAT? A SANGWITCH! NA, NA! I'LL GIE YE BREED AN' CHEESE, AN' AS MUCH WHUSKEY AS YE CAN DRINK; BUT, TAE MAK' SANGWIDGES ON THE SAUBBERTH DAY!"——

23, 24   *Punch* cartoons, 1870

25   Illustration to a Temperance story, 1896: 'She caught them up, one in either hand, and held them as high as she could lift them. "If you don't sit down and promise to keep still, I'll smash them both on the hearth"'

21, 22   Cutting peat for the kilns (cf. plate 29) and transporting whisky to the railway station, 1890

26   Postcard illustration by Donald McGill:
'It's just a common sore throat. Gargle it with a little whisky'
'An' would it dae me any harm if a wee drop happens tae trickle doon, Doctor?'

capture seemed inevitable . . . pretending to surrender he invited the gaugers into his boat to take possession, and seized one of their oars to assist them in stepping on board. In a twinkle he had thrown the oar on top of his potheen barrels and quickly rowed downstream, leaving the poor discomfited gaugers with but one oar. . . . He was soon lost to sight and landed his cargo safely.

In his *Wild Sports and Natural History of the Highlands* Charles St. John, the sportsman, naturalist and author recounted how, along with his servant Donald, he was benighted on a wild, wet, dark night in the Morayshire hills in 1845, while in pursuit of a great stag, the famed 'Muckle Hart of Benmore'. He was forced to spend the night eventually in a 'whiskie bothie' which he traced by the sound of wild fiddling coming apparently out of the darkness ahead. He gave Donald's explanation of the phenomenon and then recounted the scene:

'It's all right enough, sir, just follow the sound; it's that drunken deevil, Sandy Ross; ye'll never haud a fiddle frae him, nor him frae a whisky still'. . . . Following the merry sound we came to what seemed a mere hole in the bank, from which it proceeded. The hole was partially closed by a door woven of heather. . . . On a barrel in the middle of the apartment – half hut, half cavern – stood aloft, fiddling with all his might, the identical Sandy Ross, while round him danced three unkempt savages; and another figure was stooping, employed over a fire in the corner, where the whisky pot was in full operation. The fire, and a sliver or two of lighted bog fir, gave light enough to see the whole, for the place was not above ten feet square. We made our approaches with becoming caution, and were, needless to say, hospitably received; for who ever heard of Highland smugglers refusing a welcome to sportsmen? We got rest, food and fire – all we required – and something more; for long after I had betaken me to the dry heather in the corner, I had disturbed visions of strange orgies in the bothie, and of my sober Donald exhibiting curious antics on the top of a tub . . . when daylight awoke me, the smugglers and Donald were all quiet and asleep, far past my efforts to arouse them, with the exception of one who was still able to tend the fire under the large black pot. From the state in which my trusty companion was, with his head in a heap of ashes I saw it would serve no purpose to wake him, even if I were able to do so. It was quite clear he would be good for nothing all day. I therefore . . . departed with my rifle alone. . . .

The days of such scenes were nearly over, however, for already Queen Victoria had begun her search for her Highland estate. Soon the Royal Family was to move to Balmoral and set the fashion for the English to buy estates in the Highlands, or else take annual Highland holidays. Under her aegis the Highlands suddenly became respectable. Already the mecca of the fisherman and shooting man, the sportsman after salmon, grouse or deer, they were now to suffer an annual influx of tourists as well.

In the hundred years between 1745 and 1845 immense changes had taken place in the Highlands. The formation of eighty-six Highland regiments had drained much of their manpower. As early as 1762 sheep were introduced by Admiral Sir John Lockhart, a Lowlander who had inherited a Highland estate. They were soon being introduced everywhere and whole townships were being razed to the ground to make way for them. Ironically, very often the chieftain who thus mercilessly evicted his own clansmen was subsequently bought out and dispossessed by a Lowlander or Englishman; alternatively his estates were frequently inherited by English or Lowlanders through marriage.

Thousands upon thousands of Highlanders, thus evicted, emigrated to the New World, often in appalling conditions, to make a new life for themselves. The Clearances were a painful and shameful period. Amongst the worst, perhaps, were those in Sutherland, all the worse for being totally unnecessary, supervised by a Lowlander who did not understand the Highlanders or their way of life. The Duke, himself descended from Yorkshire mill and coal owners, was hardly of Highland stock. As the Highlanders were dispossessed the Lowlanders or English moved in, adopting the tartan and the way of life to suit themselves.

By 1848 the old ways had not entirely vanished. In the charter room at Blair Castle there is a petition from the Duke of Athol's tenants in Strathtummel. The petitioners pointed out that they had managed to pay their rents, not by farming but by illicit distilling. Now, despite the failure of their potato crop, they considered they might still be able to pay their rents if 'His Grace's assistance could be so managed that the stringency of the excise laws . . . could be although only partially removed. The petitioners did not want any legislative enactment for accomplishing this, the mere removal of the District officer . . . would . . . be sufficient'.

Among the enterprising distillers who had followed George Smith's example and taken advantage of the 1823 Act was John Robertson, who had founded a distillery below the mountain of Lochnagar, close to Balmoral. Known as the Lochnagar distillery, it was bought by John Begg in 1845. On the 12th of September 1848 he received a visit from the Royal Family, which he duly chronicled at length in his journal:

I wrote a note on the 11th September to Mr. G. E. Anson (Her Majesty's Private Secretary) stating that the distillery was now in full operation, and would be so until six o'clock next day, and, knowing how anxious H.R.H. Prince Albert was to patronize and make himself acquainted with everything of a mechanical nature, I said I should feel much pleasure in showing him the works. The note was handed in at Balmoral Castle about 9 p.m. Next day about four o'clock, whilst in the house, I observed Her Majesty and the Prince Consort approaching. I ran and opened the door, when the Prince said, 'We have come to see through your works, Mr. Begg'. There were besides, T.R.H. the Prince of Wales, the Princess Royal, and Prince Alfred, accompanied by Lady Cumming. I at once conducted the Royal Party to the distillery. On entering the works, the two young Princes at once ran away among the casks, like any other children, whereupon Her Majesty called them, 'Where are you young children going?' on which I laid hold of one in each hand and held them during the time they remained. I endeavoured to explain the whole process of malting, brewing and distilling, showing the Royal Party the bere [barley] in its original state, and in all its different stages of manufacture until it came out at the mouth of the still pipes. On going downstairs H.R.H. turned round to me and said (looking at the locks on the stills) 'I see you have got your locks there'. On my replying, 'These are the Queen's locks,' Her Majesty took a hearty laugh. When we came to the door I asked H.R.H. if he would like to taste the spirit in its matured state, as we had cleared some that day from Bond, which I thought was very fine. H.R.H. having agreed to this, I called for a bottle and glasses (which had previously been in readiness) and, presenting one glass to Her Majesty, she tasted it. So also did His Royal Highness the Prince. I then presented a glass to the Princess Royal, and to the Prince of Wales and Prince Alfred, all of whom tasted the spirit. H.R.H. the Prince of Wales was going to carry his glass quickly to his mouth. I checked him, saying it was very strong, and so he did not take but a very small drop of it. Afterwards the Royal Party took their departure, I thanking them for the honour of the visit they had been so generous to pay the distillery.

Scarcely surprisingly, after this visit, John Begg was appointed distiller to the Queen, by royal warrant. He was also empowered to call his distillery the Royal Lochnagar Distillery. Admittedly he made a good whisky, but it is questionable whether in fact it was as outstanding as it was made out to be thereafter by those claiming to be connoisseurs.

Meanwhile in Glenlivet another distillery had been built by Captain William Grant, officer in charge of the troops supporting the Excise against illicit distilling, who had married George Smith's daughter Margaret. He had now settled down at Auchorachan on the opposite side of the glen to his father-in-law and started distilling. It is clear, however, that already they were suffering from a number of other distilleries capitalising on the fame of the name Glenlivet and selling their whisky under that name. In 1849 he wrote to Messrs. Hay in Edinburgh, the agents for his landlord, the Duke of Richmond and Gordon, enclosing the following announcement:

Glenlivet Whiskey
Captain William Grant of the Aorachan Distillery *Glenlivet* begs to acquaint Connoisseurs in whiskey, that in that far flung Glen, which wholly belongs to the Duke of Richmond, there is no other Distillery than *his own* and that of *George Smith of the Drumin Glenlivet* Distillery, – nor within several miles of it and the Public is respectfully cautioned against any other Distillery assuming that title.   Glenlivet 8th November 1849.

The accompanying letter beneath this announcement read:

Captain Grant will be much obliged to Messrs. Hay and Coy to get the above inserted in the North British Advertiser twice and twice in any one or two of such Glasgow Papers as they may approve, for which the Captain will pay. The Captain will feel obliged by Messrs. Hay seeing that he gets the North British Advertiser sent him regularly as having two Distilleries and paying about £400 a year rent he thinks these arrangements will allow them to send it gratis.

The insertion of such advertisements and the royal approval given to whisky must have shocked the stern supporters of the Temperance Movement. Among the leaders of these was Lord Provost Duncan M'Laren of Edinburgh, author of a pamphlet published by the Scottish Temperance League, entitled *Whisky Drinking in Scotland*. With the publication of statistics prepared by the Editor of *The Scotsman*, which indicated that 'Glasgow was three times more drunken than Edinburgh and five times more so than London', public opinion was moved to approve action. Under the Forbes Mackenzie Act of 1853 much stricter opening hours were imposed on licensed premises.

The same year, 1853, saw a further Act passed by Gladstone's government, which had far-reaching effects on all distilleries. For the convenience of Excise officers the spirit safe, duly padlocked, through which the newly distilled spirit emerges from the still, was made compulsory in all distilleries. While abolishing the malt tax in Scotland for distillers, the duty was raised from 3s 8d to 4s 8d per proof gallon. This was the start of a steady upwards trend in duty during the 1850s, which was to reduce the number of malt distilleries once more. Although the Repeal of the Corn Laws in 1846 had paved the way for the importation of

EARAIL DO
OIGRIDH NA GAEDHEALTACHD.

POITEAR. Mata! mata! Agus cha'n ol thu deur de *dhruchd nam beann* ag-aibh fein!

GAEDHEAL. Cha bhuin, cha bhlais, 's cha laimhsich mi e; agus cha 'n e sin uil' e ach ni mi nas urrainn domh gu iompaidh a chur air muinntir eile fuireach uaithe mar an ceudna.

Exhortation to the Youth of Gaeldom, *a Temperance tract published in Glasgow c. 1850. The caption reads:*

TOPER. *Well! Well! And you won't drink a drop of your own* mountain dew!

GAEL. *No I won't, I won't taste it, nor will I handle it; and not only that but I'll do everything in my power to persuade people to stay away from it in like fashion*

cheap maize from abroad for the benefit of the grain distillers in the Lowlands, they do not appear to have started using it for a decade or more.

The following year, 1854, saw the outbreak of the Crimean War and once again the Highlands were combed for volunteers to fight, but on this occasion the results were disappointing. When the second Duke of Sutherland addressed a specially summoned meeting of some four hundred men in the village of Golspie he explained the necessity of defeating the Czar and the Russians. Then he called for volunteers, but not one stepped forward. When the Duke thereupon indignantly demanded the reason, according to Donald MacLeod's *Gloomy*

91

Memories of the Highlands of Scotland, one old man stepped forward and answered him as follows:

I am sorry for the response your Grace's proposals are meeting here today, so near the spot where your maternal grandmother by giving some forty-eight hours' notice marshalled 1,500 men to pick out the 800 she required, but there is a cause for it and a genuine cause and, as your Grace demands to know it, I must tell you as I see none else is inclined in the assembly to do so. These lands are now devoted to rear dumb animals which your parents considered of far more value than men. I do assure your Grace that it is the prevailing opinion of this county that, should the Czar of Russia take possession of Dunrobin Castle and Stafford House next term that we could not expect worse treatment at his hands than we have experienced at the hands of your family for the past fifty years. Your parents, yourself and your Commissioners have desolated the glens and the straths of Sutherland where you should find hundreds, yea thousands of men to meet and respond to your call cheerfully had your parents kept faith with them. How could your Grace expect to find men where they are not and the few of them that are to be found have more sense than to be decoyed off by chaff to the field of slaughter. But one comfort you have; though you cannot find men to fight, you can supply those who will with plenty of mutton, beef and venison.

A great change had indeed taken place in the Highlands. Despite the steady rise in duty during the 1850s, by 1854 seizures of illicit stills had fallen to seventy-three and within a decade the figure was to be down to nineteen. Yet in 1854 the duty was raised to 6s per proof gallon. The following year it was brought up to the English level of 8s per proof gallon, but the introduction of the Methylated Spirits Act at the same time, allowing the sale of duty-free spirits to industry, denied the illicit distiller a market for paint stripper and other industrial uses on which he had previously been able to rely. This Act also appears to have intensified the competition among the patent-still distillers for they entered into their first Trade Agreement in 1856. In the end, however, this was to give the Lowland patent-still grain distillers the lead in their long battle with the Highland pot-still malt distillers.

The 'northern gentry', as Gillespie had stated, might prefer the malt pot-still whisky to the patent-still grain whisky, but the patent-still grain distillers were able to produce much greater quantities. With the use of cheap imported maize they were also able to produce it more economically. In 1850 there was more malt whisky being produced in Scotland than grain whisky. 59.8% of the total produced was malt whisky as against 40.2% grain whisky. By 1860 the figures were nearly reversed with 57.9% of the total production being grain whisky as opposed to 42.1% malt whisky. With the final increase in duty in 1860 to 10s per proof gallon the number of malt distillers had fallen to 108 as against 139 at the start of the decade. The bulk of the working men in the country drank grain whisky, or a blend. The pattern of the future was set.

8. First Trade Arrangement 1856 to Death of Victoria 1901

Glenlivet has its castles three
Drumin, Blairfindy and Deskie,
And also one distillery
More famous than the castles three.

Traditional

The founder firms which entered into a Trade Arrangement in 1856 with a view to agreed trade allocations between them in fixed proportions were Menzies, Bernard & Craig, 41½%; John Bald & Co., 15%; John Haig & Co., 13½%; MacNab Brothers & Co., 11½%; Robert Mowbray, 10½%; and John Crabbie & Co., 8%. It was notable that all were Lowland grain distillers and at the time of the agreement their total stocks consisted of under 1,700 gallons. At this time very little was being held in bond, but was being passed on to the purchaser directly as soon as it was distilled.

A notable feature of the period up to 1860 was the steadily growing number of whisky merchants, many of them bearing names subsequently famous, not only within the industry, but internationally, as well-known trade names for whisky. Old-established firms at this time included Matthew Gloag, who had set up in Perth in 1814, to be followed by T. R. Sandeman in 1825. Meanwhile, in

1820, John Walker had opened his licensed grocer's shop in Kilmarnock, Ayrshire, and in 1841 James Chivas founded a similar firm in Aberdeen. In 1846 John Dewar formed his own business among the merchants of Perth, while among the more prominent firms in Edinburgh were those of Andrew Usher and William Hill, the latter established in 1793. In 1857 William Thomson joined William Hill at 45, Frederick Street, and the name of the firm was amended to Hill Thomson.

In 1860 Gladstone's Excise on Spirits Act remedied a long-standing injustice, whereby since 1847 the English distillers had been allowed to use sugar, mangel wurzels, potatoes, molasses, grain and malt as raw materials for brewing, whereas the Scots had been restricted to grain and malt. In addition, even more belatedly, the Act finally implemented the proposal made by the Parnell Commission in 1856 that exports of whisky from Scotland might henceforth be in bottles rather than restricted to eighty-gallon casks. This was a factor which had hitherto undoubtedly restricted exports considerably and, with the relaxation of this prohibition, sales, especially to England, steadily increased.

The new freedom somewhat compensated for the additional 2s on the Excise duty which the Act also imposed. By this time the annual production of grain whisky exceeded that of malt whisky by 5.8% (6,886,478 gallons of grain spirit as opposed to 5,017,525 of malt), but this *status quo* was not to alter greatly over the next two decades. During this period there was little sign of the boom that was to come in the eighties and nineties of the century and most distillers were merely struggling along on the verge of bankruptcy.

At this stage virtually no distillers sold their own whisky other than in casks, the favourite size being the ten-gallon anker, which was comparatively easy to transport, especially by horse, still the only means of transport from many of the more remote Highland distilleries. Both bottling and blending were almost entirely the province of the whisky merchants, who had gradually become increasingly important customers, sometimes buying what amounted to an entire distillery's output. They thus began to have a powerful influence on the industry.

As early as 1822 Elizabeth Grant mentioned in her *Memoirs* that it had been customary for the more discriminating whisky drinkers to mature their spirit in the barrel. It had already been appreciated that when kept in a cask for a period of years whisky matured in mellowness and flavour, whereas when bottled virtually no further change took place. No doubt it was not long before the further discovery was made that an old sherry barrel was ideal for the purpose, imparting a slight colouring to the spirit in the process. Knowledge of such matters was part of the merchant's essential background, as much as his skill and judgement in assessing the public taste and catering for it, on which his survival depended. In the latter instance his ability to assess the flavour of the various malt whiskies, both Highland and Lowland, and his skill in blending them were all important.

It was the merchants' custom, first attributed to Andrew Usher of Edinburgh in 1853, to blend the Highland malt whiskies with their strong individual flavours to achieve the most satisfactory appeal to the public taste. This was termed a 'blended' whisky. A skilful blend of the strong Highland malt whiskies and the generally milder Lowland malt whiskies was regarded by many merchants as providing the most saleable blended whisky. When malt and grain whisky were combined the trade description at first was simply a 'mixture'. Yet it was soon discovered that such a mixture was more reliably stable than a blend of malts.

After the Spirits Act of 1860 permitted blending of spirits in bond the wholesalers, or merchant blenders, began to take advantage of their opportunity to produce a cheaper and less variable blend by mixing malt with grain whiskies. By degrees the distinction became blurred and by the 1870s the term blend had come to be generally accepted as a mixture of malt and grain whiskies as well as malt whiskies blended with malt whiskies. During the same decade the amount of whisky in bonded warehouses in Scotland almost trebled, for as the demand for more mature whisky developed the merchants were able to insist on the distillers holding stocks in bond at their own cost. This was an imposition which the distillers naturally resented, but they were not sufficiently organised amongst themselves to be able to resist it effectively. The malt pot-still distillers were particularly affected by this pressure from the merchants, but individualists to a man they had yet to learn the importance of combining and presenting a common front.

Although a number of malt distillers had suffered during the 1850s, due to the steady increase in duty, others, the Glenlivet distillery in particular, had gone from strength to strength. Following the death of Captain William Grant, the Auchorachan distillery had been closed, but in 1850 George Smith had opened another distillery at Delnabo near Tomintoul, known as the Cairngorm distillery. With this and the Upper Drumin distillery he was still unable to meet the demand for the Glenlivet whisky and between 1858 and 1861 in conjunction with his son John Gordon Smith, now in partnership with him, a new distillery was built at Minmore producing six hundred gallons a week. The old distilleries were scrapped.

The pack-horse train, which had carried the barrels of whisky the thirty-five miles to the coast had by this time been replaced by carts drawn by Clydesdales, but even so it was a long haul. When the new railway line reached Ballindalloch in 1863, only seven miles from the distillery at Minmore, it eased the difficulties of transport immediately. It is significant that Andrew Usher & Co., who had been agents for the Glenlivet distillery since 1840, started exporting for them in 1864.

It is an indication of the lack of co-operation between the malt distillers that the Smiths clearly still suffered greatly from the distilleries for many miles around who continued to trade on the known excellence of the name Glenlivet, as is shown by a letter signed by the Duke of Richmond and Gordon:

> November 6. 1865.
> The District of Glenlivet, a
> part of the Gordon property
> in Scotland belongs to me
> My tenants George and
> John Gordon Smith, whose
> distillery of malt Whiskey
> is called "The Glenlivet"
> "Distillery" – are the only
> distillers in the Glenlivet
> district—
> Richmond.

Among the grain distillers the first Trade Arrangement lasted for nine years before being concluded due to internal dissatisfaction. A new Trade Arrangement promptly followed, in 1865, with the firm of John Crabbie & Co. replaced by Macfarlane & Co. Further arrangements were agreed with the Irish distillers and after a threat of all-out trade war an arrangement was also finally agreed with the English distillers, so that by 1867 the price of grain spirit reached an all-time high, leaping from 1s 7d per proof gallon to 2s 7d. Even so, it often seemed as if the apathy of members and the lack of organised control would end in this second Trade Arrangement also being discontinued. Yet the importance of whisky in Scotland may be gauged from the fact that in 1870 the annual consumption of spirits per head was twenty-three pints, whereas in England it was a mere seven. It is not perhaps really surprising that the extreme Temperance supporters were advocating Prohibition on the lines already introduced in the State of Maine in 1851.

This was a period when associations were being formed throughout the industry. The Campbeltown and Islay distillers had an informal association and the Elgin Distillers Association represented the distillers within the Elgin Excise control. In 1874 this latter association decided that, in view of the keen competition in the industry, 'it is highly desirable to form a strong Association of Distillers'. Excluding the southern distillers and those in Islay and Campbeltown, who already had associations, they decided to concentrate on the distillers 'North of the Grampians'. At their inaugural meeting the name chosen was 'The North of Scotland Malt Distillers' Association' and membership included thirty-six of the forty-nine distilleries in the chosen area, including Talisker on Skye and the Highland Park Distillery in Orkney.

The principal aim of this association was to attempt to gain a better bargaining position with the buyers of their whisky, the merchants who bought their production in bulk. One of their chief objects was to get the buyer to share part of the cost of warehousing the whisky in bond while it was maturing, for, as noted, the demand for mature spirit was steadily increasing so that the amount in bond by 1880 had almost trebled in the decade. Otherwise the association was agreed to resist any attempt at increasing Excise duty and to oppose the Temperance Movement, both broad aims approved by the entire industry.

It was obvious that loose-knit associations were not a sufficient answer to the problems facing the industry. In 1875 Mr. Robert Stewart of Kirkliston Distillery, West Lothian, although not himself a member of the second Trade Arrangement, put forward a proposal, together with his accountant Mr. Alexander Moore, for the formation of a powerful limited company composed of the principal firms among the Scottish grain distillers. The advantages of centralisation of control, of buying and selling, of avoiding interference, and of regulating supply were all points put forward in favour of the move. The fact that there was an influx of cheap German spirit at this stage probably helped to swing members in favour of the proposal, in addition to its patently obvious advantages. After discussing it and agreeing in favour there was a further six months' delay before action was taken.

It was not eventually until April 24th 1877 that the new company was formed, to be known as the Distillers Company Ltd., with a nominal capital of £2,000,000, divided into 40,000 shares of £50 each, although only 12,000 shares were issued to the six firms involved. These were John Bald & Co., Carsebridge Distillery, Alloa; John Haig & Co., Cameron Bridge Distillery, Fife; M. Macfarlane & Co., Port Dundas Distillery, Glasgow; MacNab Bros & Co., Glenochil Distillery, Menstrie; Robert Mowbray, Cambus Distillery, Alloa; Stewart & Co., Kirkliston Distillery, West Lothian. Known latterly simply by the initials D.C.L. this was to become the most powerful force in the Scotch whisky industry.

An Edinburgh lawyer, Mr. W. S. Fraser, of the Edinburgh legal firm of Fraser, Stoddart and Ballingal, who represented the new Company, referred in a speech to the various directors, whom he knew intimately, as 'the determined Haig, the politic Bald, the impetuous Macfarlane, the subtle Mowbray, the

Smuggling in Scotland, 1891

99

Illicit distilling in Scotland, 1891

anxious Stewart, the cautious MacNab and the bold Menzies'. Since this was the amalgam of qualities hammered into the Scots character by Edward I which produced the Declaration of Arbroath, it augured well for the new company, once they had learned to work in harmony together.

In 1880 the Malt Tax, source of so much bitterness after the Union, was finally repealed. This measure was welcomed by the industry but not by the Excisemen since it resulted in a belated upsurge in illicit distilling. As making malt was no longer illegal in itself it meant that the Excise officers had to catch an illicit distiller at work while actually brewing or distilling, a period lasting only between four and six days, instead of about three weeks. However, the high standard of legal distilling by this time ensured that the cruder illicit product was harder to sell and resulted in the revival of the illicit trade being a brief one.

The same year, 1880, saw an interesting legal decision on the subject of the use of the title 'The Glenlivet' whisky. For a long time Glenlivet had been known sarcastically as the longest glen in Scotland because of the many distillers who claimed that they were selling Glenlivet whisky. In at least one case the distillery was over twenty miles from the glen itself, but continued to use the name which had become synonymous with the best malt whisky ever since the days of the original John Smith.

John Gordon Smith, son of George Smith, who had taken over the distillery at Minmore on the death of his father at the age of seventy-nine in 1871, having had a legal training, decided to put the matter to the courts. He claimed that his was the only distillery in the glen and that as a consequence he was the only one entitled to use 'The Glenlivet' as a trade name. The verdict of the court was that he was indeed the only one entitled to label his whisky 'The Glenlivet', but that other distilleries might use the name Glenlivet hyphenated with their own. It is a measure of the excellence of the whisky concerned and the magic of the name that by a legal agreement reached in 1884 some eighteen distilleries decided to do so and in the end the number reached twenty-five.

In 1885 Gladstone's Liberal government proposed an additional 2s duty on spirits. The object of the increase was to raise sufficient revenue to finance an expeditionary force to put down the Mahdi's rebellion in Egypt, which had resulted in the fall of Khartoum and General Gordon's death. The Chancellor of the Exchequer, however, would not agree, as he had to a similar proposed increase on the duty on beer, to the tax being purely for the duration of the war.

The Scots 'whisky' lobby in the House of Commons was joined by the Irish M.P.s, ever eager to support the Irish distilling and brewing interests, as well as by the powerful 'gin' supporters in the south. A member for Glasgow produced a petition against the proposal signed by 72,000 names and the suggestion was made that the proposed tax would result in the introduction of German spirit 'fit only for lighting lamps'. The Conservative members also used the occasion to attack the government's entire foreign policy. In the ensuing vote the government was defeated by twelve votes and the following morning Gladstone resigned from office. On a previous occasion, when defeated by Disraeli in the 1874 election, Gladstone had subsequently claimed that he had been 'borne down by a torrent of gin and beer'. No doubt on this occasion he would have put whisky first.

By this time the Scotch whisky boom was already beginning and there was to be a vast expansion of sales in the two decades from 1880 onwards. On the continent the deadly *Phylloxera vastatrix*, an insect which attacks the roots of vines, had spread throughout France during the 1870s despite all efforts to check its progress. It had finally devastated the vineyards of the Grande Champagne in the heart of the Cognac area. As a result the stocks of brandy were reduced to a minimum. The English who had hitherto relied on brandy as their after-dinner drink were ready for a substitute. Blended Scotch whisky was on hand and the men to sell it were also available. The 1880s and '90s were to see a succession of brilliant Scots whisky salesmen taking London by storm.

First in the field was James Buchanan, who initially went to London as agent for Charles Mackinlay the blenders and merchants in 1879. In 1884 he set up on his own, with little more than his superb ability as a salesman behind him. Tall, lean, handsome and red-haired, always faultlessly dressed in a frock coat, with a top hat and malacca cane, he had both presence and charm. Choosing a light blend, suitable to southern tastes, he named it Buchanan's and marketed it in a bottle with a neat black-and-white label. As his accountant was the chairman of the United Music Halls, he first opened up outlets in the music halls. He soon followed this with further outlets in the licensed trade and within a year he had obtained a contract to supply the House of Commons with his whisky. Very soon his 'Black and White' whisky was on sale all over London.

In 1880 the firm of John Walker opened up a London office. The original small merchant's business John Walker had set up in the manufacturing town of Kilmarnock in 1820 had survived various vicissitudes until Alexander joined his father in the business in 1857. With a sound business training in Glasgow behind him and with considerable vision he turned from purely local retail sales to wholesale trading and exporting. To start with he made a point of attracting the custom of the English visitors to the industries for which Kilmarnock was then famous, notably carpet manufacturing, knitted goods and lace-curtain production. Through these visitors he slowly but steadily built up a London trade.

He also developed considerable overseas trade by a system then currently known as 'Merchant Adventure Business', whereby merchants and manufacturers combined to make up a suitable cargo for a merchant ship. This would be sold at an overseas port at the best available prices by the captain or an agent for the ship's owners, who deducted their agreed percentage for transport and services from the profits. In this way the merchants and manufacturers saved the considerable expense of employing agents abroad, or of going abroad themselves. It may not have been the best way of selling whisky but the firm of John Walker prospered. Whereas in 1856 the premises comprised a single cellar sixty feet long as a bonded store, within a decade sales had passed the 100,000 gallon mark annually and a new warehouse had to be built.

In 1880 Alexander, by this time in sole charge of the firm, opened his office in London at 3, Crosby Square. At that time, when most businessmen were accustomed to travel in hansom cabs, to attract attention he made a point of driving everywhere in a specially built phaeton drawn by a perfectly matched pair of horses. His showmanship paid off and the orders for John Walker's whisky continued to rise. In 1886 Alexander was able to take his sons George and John into the business and turn it into a private limited company in the name of John Walker & Sons Limited.

If James Buchanan and Alexander Walker had succeeded in attracting attention and selling whisky successfully it was the Dewar brothers, John Alexander and Thomas Robert, who really started making Londoners Scotch whisky conscious. Their business had similar humble beginnings to that of John Walker. Their father, John Dewar, son of a Perthshire crofter, started in 1826 as assistant to a cousin named Macdonald, a wine and spirit merchant in Perth. By 1837 he was a partner, but by 1846 he decided to set up in business on his own. He was among the first to put whisky in bottles and sell it by the bottle rather than the cask. In 1879 he took his son John Alexander, then aged 23, into partnership. In 1880 he died leaving John Alexander in charge of the business. In 1884 Thomas Robert, then aged 21, joined his brother and they agreed to take the gamble of trying to expand their business by setting up a London office.

A dapper, witty young Scot, Tommy Dewar was a volcanic salesman. During a brief visit to the Brewer's Show in 1884 he had noticed that musical boxes were common at many of the stands. When he attended the show the following year he took his bagpipes. The blast of the pipes deafened all his competitors and the President and Committee were furious, ordering him peremptorily to stop at once. He retorted that bagpipes were preferable to musical boxes and played on more loudly than ever. He was nearly thrown out, but the Press loved it and he gained the headlines he required. The orders immediately began to flow in and the Dewar brothers' fortunes were founded. Soon the House of Dewar was famous.

Despite their successes it was not all easy going for these Scottish whisky pioneers. There was still considerable resistance to the Scots in England and a classic example of this was the difficulties the Distillers Company Limited encountered in trying to get their shares quoted on the London Stock Exchange. Although their initial application was made in January 1884 it was not finally successful until October 1886.

One English stockbroker in particular, a Mr. Gundry, seemed to regard it as his mission in life to prevent the D.C.L. application from being accepted. He did all he could to block it by raising objection after objection and exasperated the Company's lawyers, Messrs. Fraser, Stoddart and Ballingal. Towards the close of their voluminous correspondence Mr. Gundry ended one letter to the lawyers with the comment that, if this was an example of Scottish law, 'I thank God I am not a Scotsman'. He received the prompt reply: 'Messrs. Fraser, Stoddart and Ballingal acknowledge receipt of Mr. Gundry's letter . . . and join with him in thanking God he is not a Scotsman'.

Nor were the English alone in opposing the D.C.L. In Scotland the Press raised the question of undue monopoly and in 1888 a number of Scots grain distillers not included in the company formed their own rival company, the North British Distillery Company, which had a capacity of between two and three million gallons of spirit a year. By this time, however, the D.C.L. was already developing strongly and they were soon expanding even more. In the next decade they began their policy of buying up distilleries and building new ones, both malt and grain, as well as opening up new markets abroad and experimenting with outside interests, notably the manufacture of yeast.

The steady increase in the power of the wholesale blenders and the grain-spirit distillers was by this time causing considerable alarm amongst the malt-whisky distillers. As early as 1885 John Harvey, of the Dundas Hill distillery in Glasgow, Chairman of the West and South of Scotland Malt Distillers Association, which included twenty-nine distilleries, had approached Donald McDonald, Chairman of the North of Scotland Malt Distillers Association, with a view to forming a Central Association of Malt Distillers of Scotland. Donald McDonald, of the Ben Nevis distillery, had agreed in principle, but wanted to see it on a broader basis including grain distillers, wholesale blenders and retailers, thus representing the industry at all levels. Such a suggestion, however, was too far ahead of its time and nothing came of it.

In 1887, nevertheless, Donald McDonald, speaking at the A.G.M. of his Association, expressed publicly the feelings of his Committee:

. . . As the interests of the Highland Malt Distillers are meantime being so far sacrificed to that of the blenders your Committee think some steps should be taken either through local members of Parliament or otherwise to get the present system thoroughly exposed – so that the public may have some guarantee in buying 'Highland Malt' that they get this in reality and not as at present in many cases a mixture of three-quarters of raw grain.

There can be no question that the present sale of much so called 'Highland Malt' is little better than a fraud and it seems to your Committee that the exposure of this is due not merely for trade purposes but in [the interests] of the public.

. . . Unless some stop is put to this practice the present demand for Scotch Highland Whisky will be seriously interfered with . . . much of the pernicious stuff . . . now being palmed off as such . . . never passed through a pot still . . . consequently giving a false impression to the consumer of what genuine Highland Malt Whisky is. . . .

Eventually, after balking at the legal costs of a test case in the courts, the Association succeeded in having the matter raised in the House of Commons in 1889 and a select Committee was appointed in 1890 under the Chairmanship of Sir Lyon Playfair.

To consider whether on grounds of public health, it is desirable that certain classes of Spirits, British and Foreign, should be kept in Bond for a definite period before they are allowed to pass into consumption, and to enquire into the system of blending British and Foreign Spirits in or out of bond, and into the propriety of applying the Sale of Food and Drugs Act and the Merchandise Marks Act to the case of British and Foreign Spirits.

There were various attempts before the appointment of the Committee to reach agreement amongst the grain and malt distillers on a united approach to such matters as compulsory bonding and blending, but except for a general objection to the import of foreign spirits no common ground could be found. The grain and malt distillers approached the Committee still violently opposed to each other.

In the event the Committee only called twenty-six witnesses and failed entirely to come to any useful conclusions. Their report read in part:

Your Committee do not attempt a legal definition of whiskey [the customary spelling at this time]. . . . Whiskey is certainly a spirit consisting of alcohol and water, with a small quantity of bye-products coming from malt or grain, which give it a peculiar taste and aroma. It may be diluted with a certain quantity of water without ceasing to be whiskey, and it may be diluted with spirits containing little of the bye-products to suit the pocket and palate of the customers, and it still goes by the popular name of whiskey. Your Committee are unable to restrict the use of the name as long as the spirits added are pure and contain no noxious ingredients. . . .

Your Committee do not recommend any increased restrictions on blending spirits. . . . The addition of patent-still spirits . . . may be viewed rather as a dilution than an adulteration. . . .

Our general conclusion from the evidence submitted to us is that compulsory bonding of all spirits for a certain period is unnecessary and would harass trade. . . .

This was the period of the whisky boom at its height and nothing, it seemed, could be allowed to interfere. Between 1887 and 1899 a considerable number of malt distilleries were bought, built, re-built, or simply expanded to keep pace with the rising demand for blended whisky. Prominent amongst those built was the Glenfiddich distillery, which was actually built in 1887 by the founder, William Grant, with his own hands and manned at first by his sons while studying for various professions. In 1891, already successful, William Grant also built Balvenie distillery in addition to Glenfiddich.

By 1895 Dufftown-Glenlivet and Longmorn-Glenlivet had been built and named as a further tribute to the high value put on the name Glenlivet. In 1896 the Glenlivet distillery itself added two new stills to cope with the increased demand. According to Alfred Barnard in his *Whisky Distilleries of the United Kingdom* the distillery was then capable of producing 234,000 gallons annually. In the same year John Dewar built a malt distillery at Aberfeldy and in 1899 Dallasmore, Knockando and Kennethmont were the last boom-period distilleries to be built.

Already many well-known brand names had appeared in the whisky trade and in less than a decade had grown internationally famous. Buchanan's Black and White, Dewar's, Haig's, Hill Thomson's Queen Anne, Mackie's White Horse, Sanderson's Vat 69, Teacher's and Johnnie Walker, were all well known by the 1890s. In 1895 Arthur Bell changed the name of Sandeman's of Perth, which by then he owned, to Arthur Bell and Sons and another familiar name appeared on the scene.

One of the prominent whisky-blending firms of this period was Pattison's Limited, run by two brothers, Robert and Walter Pattison. Starting as a firm of dairy wholesalers in Leith in the 1880s they had branched into whisky. By dint of the all too common practice of selling raw grain whisky worth $11\frac{1}{2}$d a gallon with minute quantities of malt whisky added to it as 'good Glenlivet' worth 8s 6d a gallon they achieved considerable success. Their business methods were as flamboyant as they were dubious. At one point they distributed five hundred grey parrots trained to say 'Drink Pattison's Whisky' to selected licensed grocers. They maintained a decorative houseboat on the Thames at Henley to impress their London customers and lived in ostentatious opulence. In December 1898 they failed with a deficiency of £82,000. Investigation revealed fraud, as well as their method of blending, and Robert, the senior brother, received eighteen months' imprisonment, while Walter received nine.

Following the Pattison crash the whisky boom came to an abrupt halt. The outbreak of the Boer War in 1899 was probably another contributory factor, but the plain truth was that the industry had over-expanded and a period of recovery was required. Of more significance to the industry ultimately than the Boer War was the formation in the same year of the United Yeast Co. Ltd., as a subsidiary of the D.C.L. In the First World War this was to be of considerable importance.

With the death of Victoria in 1901 it seemed the new century had really begun and the old was finally closed. Although agriculture had slumped from the 1870s onwards, whisky had remained a prominent industry in Scotland. The heavy industries, coal-mining, ironworks and ship-building were booming, but whisky had taken a place of comparable importance to the Scottish economy. Having begun the century as one of the greatest tax headaches to the government, the industry had become a very profitable venture providing enormous sums in revenue.

9. Home Consumption 1900 to Chamberlain's 1919 Budget

Freedom and Whisky gang thegither,
Tak aff your *dram*!

The Author's Earnest Cry and Prayer . . .,
ROBERT BURNS 1785/6

In the whisky industry the period from 1900 to 1930 was one of almost un-relieved downward trends. Yet this was generally the result of outside influences rather than the fault of the industry itself. In 1900 consumption of home-produced spirits achieved an unprecedented height of 37.1 million proof gallons and by 1932 it had fallen to 8.1 million proof gallons. In 1898 15.7 million proof gallons of malt whisky were distilled whereas in 1900 it was already reduced to 10,398,231 gallons. The downward trend had started.

An immediate after-effect of the Pattison crash and subsequent trial, at which the brothers' methods of 'blending' were publicly exposed, was a renewed attempt by the malt distillers to press for a definition of whisky that excluded patent-still grain spirit. At the A.G.M. of the North of Scotland Malt Distillers

Association in 1901, soon after these revelations, the Chairman, Dr. M. Cowie of the Mortlach distillery in Dufftown, took a slightly different line, but one which was to become increasingly favoured in the industry. He stated:

The question of the Merchandise Act has again been brought before our notice by the Pattison affair and I think it is a pity something cannot be done to secure that what is called Scotch whisky should be the product of Scotland. . . .

As usual, however, there was little unanimity amongst the malt distillers themselves. On almost any question connected with whisky the difficulty was to secure any united action or approach to a problem amongst all sections of the industry. The patent-still grain distillers, though many were opposed to the increasing power of the D.C.L., could generally reach a measure of agreement on matters of policy. The same could be said of the wholesale blenders, who were usually prepared to unite in their common interests. Unfortunately the malt distillers, the oldest but weakest section of the whisky industry, could practically never agree among themselves on any point.

This lack of unanimity stood out in all their actions, as when the North of Scotland Malt Distillers Association was required to give its views on a Bill put forward by the Scottish Temperance Societies in 1901 aimed at abolishing tied houses, i.e. public houses owned by the brewers. Dr. Cowie made his views on brewers plain:

I think you will admit that the quality of whisky sold in public houses is of the most vile description. Everybody is aware of this. One brewer said to me: 'I don't want your good whisky – we don't want people to drink whisky, we want them to drink beer.' I think our greatest enemies in some parts have been the brewers. I think therefore we should petition in favour of the Bill.

Other members had sharply differing views and one argued that voting for the Bill '. . . would be a very great mistake. There is no doubt this Bill is brought forward by parties who have a feeling against the whole trade and we would be playing into their hands. . . .'

In the event the Bill was rejected by the House of Lords, but the extremely deep-seated division among the various branches of the drink trade had been clearly exposed. They were still wide open to attack by the Temperance Movement. The numerous Associations simply could not combine and present a united front.

Thus, in fact, the malt distillers took little effective action to obtain a definition of whisky, despite their profound sense of injustice. After a newspaper campaign ineffectually ventilating the old malt versus grain controversy, they tried once more to have the matter raised in Parliament. This attempt got no further than a first reading of a 'Sale of Whisky' Bill introduced in 1905 by Sir Herbert Maxwell, M.P. for Wigtownshire.

The malt distillers were seriously inhibited from open attack for fear of offending their principal customers, the wholesale blenders. It was this basic feeling of insecurity which prevented them ever combining together on any issue. The average Highland distiller was always uneasily aware at the back of his mind that if necessary the blenders could probably make do with a much higher percentage of Lowland malts to his detriment. There was also the fact that a number of malt distilleries were themselves controlled by the blenders.

Another factor was that the old deep-rooted distrust between Highlander and Lowlander still prevailed to some extent. Only the truly secure, such as Colonel John Gordon Smith of The Glenlivet distillery, could afford to speak out against grain spirit and in favour of the pot-still malt whisky as the only true original Scotch whisky, knowing full well that his product would always be in demand. Yet, if the Highlander's attitude to the Lowlander was one of distrust, in his view England was still a foreign country. As late as 1904 it was stated of William Grant & Sons, makers of the noted Glenfiddich: 'Messrs. Wm. Grant & Sons do a large export trade with England, the United States and Canada'. Small wonder that the Highland malt distillers did not press for a definition of whisky in these circumstances.

Then abruptly the entire issue was brought to the fore once more by the entirely unexpected and unlikely intervention of the Labour-controlled Islington Borough Council, which had a strong Temperance bias. In 1904 the Council had successfully prosecuted several publicans and off-licences under Section 5 of the Food and Drugs Act for selling as brandy what was basically a grain spirit with brandy added to it. In 1905 they turned their attention to whisky and in November at their instigation summonses were taken out against several publicans and off-licences for selling whisky 'not of the nature, substance and quality demanded by the purchaser'.

The local Off-Licence Association, several of whose members were being prosecuted, having fought and lost the actions on brandy the previous year at a cost of over £1,000 had no funds left to defend the case. They appealed for assistance to the Edinburgh and Glasgow Wholesale Dealers Associations and the Scottish Grain Distillers, who held a meeting in the offices of the D.C.L. It was not felt to be a serious matter and the arrangements for the defence were left chiefly to the D.C.L. It is significant of the attitude of mind of the patent-still distiller towards the pot-still distillers that William Ross, Managing Director of the D.C.L., subsequently revealed in his *Memoirs*:

It was felt that the case was simply another attempt by certain pot still distillers to gain a supremacy over their patent still confreres by means of the Court – a supremacy which they had hitherto failed to effect by legislation or otherwise. . . .

The case opened in November under the magistrate of the North London Police Court, Mr. Fordham. The division between pot-still malt distillers and patent-still grain distillers was made amply clear as more and more technical evidence was called. Eventually the case did not end until February when judgement was given against the defendants, or, in other words, against patent-still grain spirit as not truly whisky within the meaning of the Food and Drugs Act. Fordham ruled:

Whisky should consist of spirit distilled in a pot still, derived from malted barley, mixed or not with unmalted barley and wheat, or either of them.

In fining the defendants 20s each with £100 costs he stated firmly:

Patent still spirit made largely from maize, has been sold as whisky in a largely increasing manner for years and the resulting product has been taken by an unsuspecting public to the benefit of the wholesale dealers and retailers and the so-called blenders have dared to concoct and place upon the market raw, new patent spirit with a mere dash of . . . Scotch whisky in it as . . . Scotch.

This decision naturally came as a considerable shock to the D.C.L. and the grain distillers, as well as to the wholesale blenders. An appeal was lodged immediately and on 25th May 1906 the case came before the only court of appeal, the Clerkenwell Quarter Sessions with Mr. W. McConnell, K.C., presiding over a bench of lay magistrates. On June 25th, after seven sittings, it became clear that the bench was equally divided on the issue and could come to no decision. The original judgement therefore remained unchanged and unconfirmed to the delight of the malt distillers and the disgust of the grain distillers, but it was obvious matters could not be left undecided in this way without a clear definition as to what constituted whisky.

111

These judgements were followed by a spate of informed and uninformed comment in the Press and public declarations by all sides, as well as a good deal of behind-the-scenes political lobbying. From the time of the Fordham decision the D.C.L. had begun to treat the affair with the utmost seriousness and now they started advertising their Cambus Grain patent-still whisky in the *Daily Mail*, offering it direct to the public with the effective selling line: 'Not a headache in a gallon'. It was symptomatic of the general insecurity of mind of the industry that the blenders first had to be reassured that the D.C.L. had no intention of entering the retail market which they regarded as their province.

At this stage the grain distillers and blenders offered a compromise by indicating that they were prepared to accept a fixed standard for the proportions of pot still and patent still required to make a blended whisky. It was Alexander Walker who induced the North of Scotland Malt Distillers Association to agree to this by pointing out that:

. . . any regulation insisting on 'Pure Malt' will be very much against the interests of the Northern Distillers. They cannot compete in price with the Southern, and where grain is not used it must be replaced with Lowland Malt of the cheapest character, and a proportion of the Highland Malt would also be displaced in order to keep the price right, so that they would stand to lose considerably by a 'Pure Malt' regulation. . . .

Alexander Walker had considerable foresight. His blends in any event had always included a high proportion of malt, but he was already deeply concerned about the common overseas practice of mixing malt whisky with local spirits and selling the product as 'Scotch' whisky. He could see the importance of ensuring that Scotch whisky production should be limited to Scotland, thus safeguarding the industry for the future, and his intervention had the effect of bringing about a mood of compromise, save for the few confirmed Highland pot-still distillers who could see no good whatever in the Lowland grain spirit.

In July 1906 a deputation led by William Ross of the D.C.L. and including both malt pot-still and grain patent-still distillers and blenders approached Mr. John Burns, President of the Board of Local Government, with a view to obtaining a Royal Commission to decide the issue. A Labour supporter turned Liberal, the first working man to attain Cabinet rank, Burns was biased against capitalists and had seen at first hand the effects of drink on the working classes in large cities. He was therefore not sympathetic to the deputation, although promising to give the matter consideration.

By 1907 no action had been taken and a general spirit of co-operation had become noticeable except amongst the most determinedly Highland pot-still distillers who still would have no truck with the Lowland patent-still distillers. A newly elected Islington Borough Council, not wishing to waste any more ratepayers' money on litigation, joined a fresh deputation to Mr. Burns in June 1907. They were received in a more reasonable manner and in July the government agreed to appoint a Royal Commission.

In February 1908 the Royal Commission began its task. The Commission was presided over by Lord James of Hereford and with him was Laurence Guillemard, the deputy chairman of the Board of Inland Revenue. The remaining six members of the Commission were all physicists or scientists. Their terms of reference were:

To consider whether in the general interest of the consumers or the interest of the public health it is desirable:

1. to place restrictions upon the materials or processes which may be used in the manufacture and preparation in the United Kingdom of Scotch and Irish whiskey or of any spirit to which the term whiskey may be applied.

2. to require a declaration of the age of whiskey and of the materials and processes used in its manufacture and to fix a minimum period during which any such spirit should be matured in bond.

The Commission sat for over seventeen months and heard 116 witnesses. The North of Scotland Malt Distillers Association put forward the view that 'Patent still spirit is not Scotch whisky except when made in Scotland and blended or mixed with 50% of Scotch malt whisky'. Others maintained that the Coffey still produced 'neutral' spirit and that the maize and similar raw materials used did not produce the same spirit as the traditional barley.

Expert witnesses were brought forward who proved that, whatever Aeneas Coffey had intended, his patent still left similar residues to the pot still, merely not in such quantity, therefore purer; also that the raw materials made no difference to the spirit produced. The grain distillers argued cogently that Cambus Grain whisky had proved acceptable to the general public, that most blends consisted of 50% malt and 50% grain and that southern tastes preferred the lighter blended whisky, which suited them better.

A little light relief in the monotonous procession of expert witnesses was afforded by the evidence of Dr. Harris, the Medical Officer of Health for Islington, who referred to a whisky made in London, which consisted of patent-still spirit mixed with a little Scotch malt pot-still whisky and sold under the initials N.S.S. The retailers refused to explain what the initials stood for in order to encourage curiosity and sales, but he was able to reveal that they meant 'Never Saw Scotland'.

The Commission issued its final findings in July 1909. They stated:

Our general conclusion . . . is that 'whiskey' is a spirit obtained by distillation from a mash of cereal grains saccharified by the diastase of malt; that 'Scotch whiskey' is whiskey, as above defined, distilled in Scotland and that 'Irish whiskey' is whiskey, as above defined, distilled in Ireland.

On the subject of bonding the Commission added: 'We have come to the conclusion that it is not desirable to require a minimum period during which spirits should be matured in bond'. This finding was directly counter to the interests of the industry, which would have preferred to have a government guarantee of age for their whisky, but otherwise it was a triumph for the grain distillers, especially the D.C.L., who had financed and organised their evidence and by doing so asserted their developing leadership.

The Commission added further satisfaction to the grain distillers' triumph by stating categorically: 'We have received no evidence to show that the form of the still has any necessary relationship to the wholesomeness of the spirit produced'. They were concerned, after all, with danger to the public health, not with taste, so that this finding was understandable enough. Combined with the rest of the report, however, it was bitterly resented by many pot-still malt distillers.

Despite the fact that the 1909 Commission's findings were condemned by many at the time and have also been condemned since as valueless, in one respect at least they were vitally important. By their definition of 'Scotch Whisky' as a whisky distilled in Scotland, a finding of legal standing subsequently incorporated into statute law (in 1952) and accepted by all other governments in the world, the Commission ensured the industry's future. It is due to this definition that the Scotch whisky industry has been able to ensure that Scotch whisky has remained the product of Scotland and has been able to prosecute any imitators in any country around the world claiming to produce 'Scotch' whisky. It is as a result of this finding that the Scotch whisky industry earns the millions of pounds in exports that it does today.

At the time this was not obvious and the Commission's findings were by no means greeted with enthusiasm in many quarters. At a dinner at Glenlivet soon after they were published the Duke of Richmond and Gordon, grandson of the Duke who had supported both the 1823 Act and the early efforts of George Smith, in a speech punctuated by laughter and applause, said firmly:

Quite recently a public enquiry has taken upon itself to decide what is whisky. And I regret to say that apparently anything that is made in Scotland, whatever its combination, is to be called Scotch whisky. For my part, I prefer, and I think that most of those whom I am addressing now, would prefer, to trust to their own palates, rather than to the dogma of chemists, and to be satisfied with the whisky that is produced in Glenlivet as against any other quality that is produced in Scotland.

Colonel John Gordon Smith, son of George Smith, had represented the old guard of the Highland pot-still malt distillers at the Commission as an independent witness. He had avowed staunchly that only whisky made in Scotland from malted barley in a fire-heated still should be termed Scotch whisky. On being questioned as to divisions amongst the pot-still malt distillers, he had claimed that the only pot-still malt distillers opposed to this definition were the minority in distilleries built during the whisky boom and controlled by the blenders. His was a gallant last stand for the Highland distillers against Lowland infiltration. It was somewhat ironic that the victory went to the blenders, for his own agents for the sale of The Glenlivet since 1840 had been Andrew Usher & Co., of Edinburgh, who had first introduced blending around 1853.

The findings of the Royal Commission were followed shortly by the 1909 Budget of the Chancellor of the Exchequer, David Lloyd George, politically a Temperance supporter. Taking advantage of the division within the industry, he seized the opportunity of raising the duty from 11s per proof gallon to 14s 9d and altering the original tax of £10 for a licence to distil to a tax on the amount distilled. Due to the lack of a united front, the tax went through without difficulty.

During the period from 1909 to 1914 the D.C.L. was particularly active in expansion. By acquiring patent-still distilleries in Ireland, Liverpool and London it effectively secured a share of the English gin and industrial-alcohol markets, as well as removing barriers for reaching agreement with the English distillers on the control and sale of methylated spirits. The formation of a subsidiary, the Industrial Spirit Supply Company, Ltd., gave it effective control of the market.

By 1912 the Chairman of D.C.L. was warning of the dangers of over-production, for the whisky industry by this time had recovered from the Pattison failure. On the verge of the 1914 war Scotch whisky exports had reached the record figure of ten million gallons, a figure not to be surpassed for twenty-six years.

In the same period the North of Scotland Malt Distillers Association for once managed to secure agreement among its members to a scheme for controlling the distribution and sale of draff, the lees of malted barley used in distilling, which was extensively used as cattle feed when dried. By this agreement members were entitled to sell their draff at a figure above the agreed minimum, but if unable to do so the Association took it over and shared any loss incurred in its sale between the members. The members thus had both guaranteed sales and a degree of independence. Furthermore the Association advertised the value of draff to farmers for animal feeding. The scheme only collapsed in 1913 because agreement could not be reached on a minimum price.

The comparative success of the agreement to sell draff underlines to some extent the degree to which the Highland distillers were still very considerably integrated with the farming of the countryside. To a great degree they still used Scottish barley and most of the old-established distillers also had farms attached to their distilleries. The Glenlivet distillery was a good example of this trend and indeed Colonel John Gordon Smith had a fine Shorthorn herd at Minmore, while his nephew Colonel George Smith Grant, his successor on his death in 1911, built up one of the most famous herds of Aberdeen Angus in the history of the breed on his farm at Auchorachan.

When it came to approving a scheme in 1912 to charge warehouse rental, however, the North of Scotland Malt Distillers Association once more found itself unable to achieve unity of action. A Committee appointed to work out a pilot scheme proposed a ten-year agreement to be signed by members binding them to charge 1d a week per eighty-gallon cask with a fine of £250 for breach of the agreement. Although thirty-six members signed the agreement, this was not sufficient to make the scheme workable and it had to be abandoned.

Throughout the period from the 1909 Budget to the outbreak of war in 1914, and indeed thereafter, the emphasis was on mergers and amalgamations with the D.C.L. continuing its policy of expansion. In every industry, in the Trade Unions, even in the Civil Service, as with the amalgamation of the Customs and Excise in 1909, the trend was towards larger groupings. In August 1914, on the eve of the war, came the amalgamation of five Lowland malt distillers into the

Scottish Malt Distillers, Ltd., with William Ross of the D.C.L. as Chairman of this D.C.L. subsidiary.

On the outbreak of the 1914 war the entire world was plunged into turmoil and nothing was ever to be quite the same again. The Scotch whisky industry was no exception. The tendency towards mergers, amalgamations and take-overs, was accelerated. Many distillers and wholesalers were unable to survive and were swallowed up, in the case of malt distillers by the newly formed Scottish Malt Distillers, Ltd., or otherwise generally by the D.C.L.

With David Lloyd George as Prime Minister, one of the government's first actions to affect the industry was the Intoxicating Liquor (Temporary Restrictions) Bill, passed in 1914 with almost no opposition, although with assurances that Prohibition would not be resorted to except in extreme emergency. By this Act the licensing hours were altered from 8 a.m. to 10 p.m. instead of the previous times of 5 a.m. to 12.30 a.m. This had the effect of achieving at a stroke most of the Temperance reformers' aims since drunkenness was immediately reduced to minimal proportions.

Surprisingly, however, it seems Lloyd George was not satisfied with this measure and seriously contemplated nationalising the entire drink industry and trade, from distillers and brewers to inns and off-licences. Fortunately saner counsels prevailed in the shape of William Ross of the D.C.L., who pointed out the countless uses of alcohol to the war effort and the importance of being able to fill the gap caused by the stoppage of supplies of yeast from Belgium. The United Yeast Co., Ltd., formed by the D.C.L. in 1899 as a subsidiary, was able to supply the yeast essential to provide the nation's supplies of bread.

As the sole remaining feature of the measures intended, the government introduced in 1915 the Immature Spirits Act, by which all spirit distilled had to be kept in bond for two years. By the end of the year the period was extended to three years. Although a measure the industry itself desired, the effect was to raise the price considerably. Combined with an acute shortage of grain and rationing of supplies to the distilleries, the outlook for many firms was bleak. Many of the malt distillers, who were unable to manufacture industrial alcohol like the patent-still distillers, were forced to close down completely, or were taken over.

The year 1915 also saw the merger of Buchanan's and Dewars, two of the companies of the 'Big Five' as they were commonly termed (that is, Buchanan, Dewar, Haig, Mackie and Walker, the only firms large enough to consider opposing the D.C.L.), which under the leadership of William Ross continued to expand. The war years, indeed, were a period of steady expansion for the D.C.L. with the take-over of firms which could not survive. The D.C.L. patent-still distilleries were also extremely busy producing industrial alcohol for many purposes connected with the war.

Under the Defence of the Realm Act Lloyd George appointed a Central Liquor Control Board with far-reaching powers. During the year 1916 it nationalised an area of fifty square miles around Carlisle. This was then an important munitions-making centre, where drunkenness was common, due to high wages, and potentially lethal. Here the Board enforced a scheme of state management and experimented with dilution of spirits, going so far as to sell spirits of only 50% proof. The scheme was also extended to an area around Invergordon in Scotland.

In 1917, amid considerable protest, the Central Liquor Control Board enforced general dilution of spirits to 30 under proof, or 70% proof. In the same year distilling was restricted to those patent-still distillers producing industrial alcohol. These and numerous other orders and restrictions resulted in the formation of the Whisky Association in the same year. The object of this Association was to form a strong central body to voice the opinions and defend the interests of all distillers, blenders and exporters. For the first time, under the exigencies of war, the industry was at last presenting a united front. In the same year, due to these restrictions and to lack of control, the price of whisky soared from 20s to 80s a gallon.

The following year produced further shocks in the shape of an increase in duty per proof gallon from 14s 9d by 15s 3d to 30s. This was imposed by Bonar Law, then Chancellor of the Exchequer, but very much inspired by Lloyd George. At the same time a system of fixed prices was instituted. The effect was to bring the trade virtually to a standstill, but somewhat naturally the increase in duty produced more revenue. This was enough for Austen Chamberlain, the next Chancellor of the Exchequer in 1919, who promptly added a further 20s to the duty, raising it to 50s per proof gallon. To strong protests from the Whisky Association against this increase he replied revealingly at one point:

As Chancellor of the Exchequer I want the biggest revenue I can get. It has always been the policy in this country to get out of alcohol . . . the largest revenue possible without stifling the Trade.

27, 28, 29 Three essential ingredients of Scotch whisky: barley, burn water and peat for the kilns (cf. plate 21)

30 Ploughing the green malt on the malting floor

31   Malt mill for crushing the dried malt into malt grist

32 Fermentation wash backs—testing a sample

33 The fermenting liquid in a wash back

LOW WINES, FEINTS & SPIRIT SAFE.

D.
INTERMEDIATE
SPIRIT RECEIVER

37   The pipe-major's reward

10. Post-War Boom in 1919 to 150th Anniversary of 'The Original Scotch' 1974

Then let us toast John Barleycorn,
    Each man a glass in hand:
And may his great prosperity
    Ne'er fail in old Scotland.

John Barleycorn, ROBERT BURNS 1787

Despite requests in 1918, it was not until early 1919 that pot-still distilling was again permitted, though even then hedged round with numerous restrictions and regulations. Regardless of these and despite the heavy increase in duty imposed that year, the whisky industry began to share in the minor boom which followed the end of the war. The introduction of Prohibition in the United States in January 1920, coupled with yet another swingeing increase in duty by 22s 6d to 72s 6d per proof gallon in Austen Chamberlain's April Budget, brought immediate protests of 'Prohibition by Price' and resulted in the boom tapering off quickly in 1921.

Exports, which had risen to over seven million gallons in 1920, dropped the following year to just over six million gallons. Even so, the price of spirits in Britain was now so high due to taxation that it was obvious the future of the industry lay in exporting. Yet these savage increases in duty also had the unfortunate effect of causing other governments overseas to raise their duties on imported spirits on the grounds that they were merely following the British government's example.

An immediate side-effect of Prohibition in the U.S.A. was a determined effort by the Temperance Movement in Britain to have a similar ban enforced. By this time, however, support and enthusiasm for the Movement was on the wane in Britain since wartime restrictions such as the limitation on licensing hours, which remained in force, as well as the vastly increased taxation on spirits, had achieved almost all they had campaigned for in the past. Furthermore the Band of Hope, the junior Temperance Movement from which the majority of its adult membership had graduated, had lost most of its supporters to the more interesting and varied activities of the Boy Scouts and Girl Guides initiated by Baden Powell. Although the notorious Prohibitionist 'Pussyfoot' Johnson came over from the United States and toured the country in 1920, he met with little success.

One of the features of the immediate post-war period which was deplored was the export of immature spirits. This was condemned on the grounds that 'The reckless shipment of practically raw whisky is bound to do the legitimate trade in the matured article incalculable harm and yet it is a practice difficult to stop without invoking fresh restrictions, of which we have had more than enough already'.

It was not long, however, before the restrictions were being withdrawn. Everyone was heartily sick of them. In 1921 the Central Liquor Control Board was disestablished, although inevitably traces of their activities remained. The Carlisle scheme, which had proved surprisingly successful, despite a deliberate policy of making drinking as uncomfortable as possible, was continued under the control of the Home Office. Although the restrictions on proof were discontinued, the trade under the overall direction of the Whisky Association decided to continue with the sale of 30 under proof whisky at a uniform price, rather than sell stronger whisky at a higher price and run the risk of being accused of making excessive profits. With the tax at 72s 6d per proof gallon it was agreed that the minimum price would have to be 16s 8d per bottle.

George Saintsbury in his *Notes on a Cellar Book* published in 1920 wrote on the effects of reducing old malt whiskies to 30 under proof with feeling. He stated categorically: 'The abominable tyranny of enforced "breaking down" to thirty below proof has spoilt the ethers of the older whiskies terribly'. Further on he described the proper way of making a toddy, which he referred to as 'almost a prehistoric compound':

Put in hot water, sweetened to taste, first and let the sugar melt thoroughly; *then* you add the whisky. And of course you do not 'swig' it brutally from the rummer or tumbler, but ladle it genteelly as required with a special instrument made and provided for the purpose into a wine glass inverted beforehands in the rummer or tumbler.

He went on to recommend the best way of keeping whisky in a cask, specifying either an 'octave' of fourteen gallons capacity or an 'anker' of ten gallons: 'Fill with good and drinkable eight year old, stand on end, tap half way up and refill when near the tap with good whisky but not too old'. He mentioned an occasion 'in a country beyond the Forth' when he complimented his host on the whisky and received the reply: 'It should be pretty good . . . it comes from a hundred gallon cask which has never been empty in a hundred years'.

It is an interesting side issue that with the return of peace it was thought there would be a reversion to selling in bulk, or by the barrel, as had been the general custom prior to 1914, rather than by the bottle, which had proved popular with the munitions workers and soldiers during the war. The usual pre-1914 practice in inns and public houses had been to sell whisky from barrels, often of glass or china, by the measure. A notable feature also was that, where these barrels were placed in front of the bar, the sales were generally much greater than where the barman, or barmaid, had to turn round to reach behind for a sale. Although these bulk sales did continue to some extent, the switch over to bottle sales was more or less complete before the end of the next decade.

Shortly after the war there was an attempt by various American interests to move into the whisky industry in Scotland. A similar attempt had been made at the time of the Pattison failure but had been thwarted by the D.C.L. On this occasion the D.C.L. interests were primarily threatened and once again they were the moving force behind the rejection of the American approach. The Fleischmann Company of New York, whose president was Mr. Julius Fleischmann, acquired a forty-eight per cent interest in the International Yeast Company of Ireland. Fleischmann's aim was to enter the British market, but by

121

acquiring financial control of the United Distillers Company of Ireland, which in turn controlled the remaining fifty-two per cent of the shares of the International Yeast Company, the D.C.L. was able to oppose the attempt. Agreement between the D.C.L. and the Fleischmann Company was probably made easier by Mr. Fleischmann's death in 1922.

The expansion of the D.C.L., which had been continuing steadily throughout the war, was a noticeable feature of the 1920s, foreshadowed in particular by the merger with Haig and Haig in 1919. Although John Haig was run as a subsidiary until 1924, it too was then finally merged with the D.C.L. Both the D.C.L. and the Scottish Malt Distillers, itself a subsidiary of the D.C.L., had been active in mergers and take-overs during the war and in the early post-war years. In 1924 the Distillers Agency, Ltd., was formed 'to acquire the blending, export and other business carried on by the Distillers Company Limited at South Queensferry, Linlithgowshire'. Thus the D.C.L., by this time a giant combine with many outside interests, arranged for a subsidiary to take control of all its export business.

Between 1925 and 1927 William Ross of the D.C.L. completed the process. In 1925 he persuaded both Walker and Buchanan-Dewar to join him in merger discussions. It was said he was the only man who could have persuaded a Walker and a Dewar to sit at the same table and the terms proposed were high, but so were the stakes. Finally the merger took place and William Ross was unanimously appointed chairman. Thereafter in 1927, after the death of Sir Peter Mackie, the D.C.L. also gained control of Mackie's White Horse Distillers, Ltd., and the 'Big Five' were thus all at last incorporated in the one vast combine.

Another important combination of interests which took place during the 1920s was amongst the Highland pot-still malt distillers. An attempt was made first in 1919 to form a combination amongst them similar to the Scottish Malt Distillers, Ltd. This, though a subsidiary of the D.C.L., was originally a combination of five Lowland malt distilleries, which had achieved considerable results by their streamlining of control and efficiency. Sharp divergencies of opinion as to the amount of compensation due to individual distillers resulted in this proposal failing.

Further attempts by the North of Scotland Malt Distillers Association to reach agreement on control of production, despite a now record number of members and increasing anxiety amongst them, failed due to mistrust of the Campbeltown and Islay distillers, whom it was feared might gain by any voluntary cut-back agreement. It was not until 1925, after extensive approaches to the Campbeltown and Islay distillers, that agreement was finally reached, not only on a voluntary restriction of 25% of output, but on the formation of a united Association. In 1926 the North of Scotland Malt Distillers Association was dissolved and the Pot-Still Malt Distillers Association of Scotland was formed.

Although it is hard to assess the exact effects of Prohibition, it can only be noted that there was a steady recession in the greater part of the Scotch whisky industry until it ended in 1933. The malt distillers in particular were gravely affected and voluntary cut-backs in production were called for increasingly by the new Association with varying degrees of success. Despite the closure of many distilleries and the take-over of many others by the Scottish Malt Distillers, Ltd., on behalf of the D.C.L., the Highland malt distillers did not take kindly to any form of regimentation or control, even when intended to be in their own interests.

Yet paradoxically it was entirely due to Prohibition that Scotch whisky achieved its dominant position of prestige in the United States. Although the principal distillers regarded the United States as a closed market and made no attempt to infringe the law, there were numerous ways in which the Americans were able to obtain Scotch whisky. In the first place, by a loophole in the law, Scotch whisky was regarded as 'of medicinal value' and considerable quantities were in fact imported on these grounds quite legitimately.

Most significant of all, however, was the sudden immense increase in exports to Canada, the British West Indies, and the Bahamas. The exports to Canada increased from 149,000 gallons in 1918 to 1,702,000 in 1920, admittedly thereafter falling to 803,000 gallons in 1922. The Bahamas were perhaps even more obvious, since the increase there was remarkable, from 944 gallons in 1918 to 386,000 gallons in 1921. The tiny French islands of St. Pierre and Miquelon, just off the Newfoundland coast, famed as bases for bootleggers, were said to have imported something like twenty gallons per head of population at one point.

Many and various were the ways in which the ban on importing Scotch whisky was overcome by thirsty Americans. In the early days bulk supplies of Scotch whisky were bought and shipped to Hamburg to be bottled and sent on from there. The Germans soon appreciated the advantages of sending their own 'neutral' spirit instead, labelled as 'Scotch' whisky. Such practices were only stopped when the firm of James Logan Mackie & Co., producers of the famed 'White Horse' blend, successfully took legal action against a merchant in Mainz for selling 'Black and White Horse Whisky' and won an important victory for Scotch whisky in the courts.

Despite the efforts of the American authorities and what amounted to a blockade by the American Navy and Coastguards, Scotch whisky continued to reach the United States in considerable quantities by one means or another throughout the 1920s. Several names were notable in connection with this trade, particularly that of Mr. James Barclay, who kept many blockade runners well supplied with Scotch. Sufficient quantities at least reached the United States to maintain its prestige and allow the Americans to acquire a taste for it, even if not sufficient to maintain the Scotch whisky industry itself in Scotland.

It was only the larger firms, the D.C.L. and the 'Big Five' within its ranks, which continued to expand successfully, if slowly in overseas markets, notably Canada and Australia, during the 1920s. For the rest of the Scotch whisky industry it was a time of continuous recession and many closures of distilleries. For the pot-still malt distillers, especially in the later 1920s, it was a harsh time indeed with many closures or bankruptcies resulting in the firms in question generally being taken over by the D.C.L., or its subsidiary the Scottish Malt Distillers, Ltd., often merely to be closed down to prevent over-production.

It was significant that the honours and wealth accumulated by the whisky industry before, during and shortly after the war were almost entirely the lot of the grain distillers. The producers of the original Scotch, the pot-still malt distillers, had no share in the honours and not a great share in the financial rewards either. The whisky barons, as they were often known, were the members of the 'Big Five' and the 1920s, or early 1930s, saw the passing of most of these colourful characters who had helped to build Scotch whisky into a world trade.

First to go was Sir Peter Mackie of the James Logan Mackie Distillers Co., Ltd., famous for their 'White Horse' blend, which he was instrumental in promoting. Known as 'Restless Peter' and sundry less printable adjectives, his motto was 'Nothing is impossible' and he had a wide range of interests beyond whisky. An active public speaker, he opposed the Lloyd George measures at every opportunity. Created a baronet in 1920 he resisted combination with the D.C.L. in his lifetime, but after his death in 1924 it was only three years before the White Horse Distillers, as they were by then known, were taken over by the combine.

Next was James Stevenson, who with Alec Walker, third generation of the

Walker family, and George Patterson Walker built up the firm of John Walker, notably by promoting the famous 'Johnnie Walker' blend from 1908 onwards. Both Stevenson and Alec Walker entered the Ministry of Munitions at Lloyd George's request during the war and Stevenson proved a genius at co-ordination. After the war he was made Lord Stevenson and Alec Walker was knighted for his services. As a result of pressure of public work, Stevenson died in 1926 at the early age of fifty-three, but Sir Alec Walker, a genial autocrat, lived on to 1950, outlasting all his contemporaries.

The most prominent of the Haig family, long connected with Lowland grain distilling and promoters of the patent still, was, of course, Field Marshal Lord Haig. He was a director of the family Cameron Bridge distillery from its formation as a public company in 1894. Despite his army career, he had the family interest in, and knowledge of, distilling. In 1922 he was made a director of the D.C.L. until his death in 1928.

Perhaps most typical of all the 'whisky barons' were the Dewar brothers. The elder, John Dewar, was Lord Provost of Perth before the turn of the century, then became an M.P. in 1907, being made Lord Forteviot of Dupplin in 1916 in recognition of his public services. The younger, irrepressible, witty Tommy Dewar, as he was widely known, became Lord Dewar in 1919. A keen sportsman, racehorse owner and coursing man, he won the Waterloo Cup in 1915 and was a member of the Jockey Club. He was chiefly famed, however, for his mastery of the witty aphorism, such as 'It's the constant advertiser who gets the trade', or 'Competition is the life of trade, but the death of profits' and countless more. The moving force behind the Dewar advertising, he died in 1930, six months after his brother.

Most distinguished of them all was James Buchanan. Tall, slim and always immaculately dressed, with perfect manners, his undoubted business genius would have taken him to the top in any sphere. Created Lord Woolavington in 1920, the apocryphal story goes that, not trusting Lloyd George, who had promised him a peerage in return for a large payment to party funds, he signed the cheque 'Woolavington'. A keen sportsman and a member of the Jockey Club along with Tommy Dewar, he had more success on the turf, winning the Derby in 1920 and again in 1926 with horses of his own breeding. Outlasting most of his contemporaries, he died in 1935 aged 86.

Yet, by any reckoning, the most outstanding, although also in many ways the most retiring, figure in the Scotch whisky industry during the formative period from around 1880 to 1930 was undoubtedly William Ross, chairman of the D.C.L. Born in 1862, he entered the D.C.L. at the age of sixteen in 1878, the year after its formation, as a junior clerk. Six foot five in height, bearded, with deep-set eyes, slim and erect, he had a keen accounting brain, enormous tact, courage and vision and by 1900 he was managing director. In many ways he was far ahead of his time, establishing a planning department in the D.C.L. long before such ideas were commonplace and ensuring that it was manned by experts in their fields. He believed firmly in the values of amalgamation and set about expanding the D.C.L. by this means with an almost religious fervour and drive. After an unfortunate shipboard accident in 1929 he went blind in 1931, dying aged 82 in 1944. To him, more than any single man, were due the changes which took place in the whisky industry in this century.

It can well be understood that men of such calibre would not descend to bootlegging during Prohibition. Yet their true attitude to Prohibition was probably best summed up by Sir Alexander Walker speaking before a Royal Commission in 1930. He was asked: 'Could you, if you would, as whisky distillers stop a large proportion of the export of liquor to the United States?' His reply was: 'Certainly not'. Indeed it was no part of the whisky distillers' intentions to indulge in bootlegging, but where their whisky went after it was sold was another matter.

The Wall Street crash in 1929 and the resulting world slump which followed probably did more than anything else to halt the flow of illegally imported Scotch to the United States. In fact it was not long thereafter before common sense prevailed, for the Americans were becoming heartily sick of the experiment. Furthermore, constant evasion was bringing the law into considerable disrepute and was doing no good to the nation. In 1932 when Franklin D. Roosevelt entered his first term of office as President he quickly sensed the mood of the country and Prohibition was repealed in 1933.

There is an apocryphal story that representatives of the 'Big Five' met each other unexpectedly on the first liner sailing for New York after the repeal of Prohibition, but, of course, the D.C.L. had made preparations well in advance, as had those wide-awake independent distillers in a position to do so. It had been obvious for some years that with the next election the law must be repealed. It was a matter of sound business sense to make all preparations possible for it beforehand.

One distiller who had been over in 1932 to investigate the American scene at first hand and make his own preparations was Captain W. Smith Grant of The Glenlivet distillery. Great-grandson of George Smith, the first licensed distiller in Scotland under the 1823 Act, grandson of Captain William Grant, who had distilled at Auchorachan on the other side of the glen, and great-great-great-grandson of John Gow, who had come over the hills and settled in the Tomintoul area after the '45, it might be fairly said that distilling was in his blood. Severely wounded as a captain in the Gordon Highlanders during the war, he took over the distillery in 1921 and worked with energy to maintain its high standards.

It is an interesting side-issue once again that it was not until 1930 that The Glenlivet distillery began bottling its own product. Until then sales had been in bulk and bottling, if carried out, had been by the buyer or agent. Of course, from about 1880 a great deal of pot-still malt whisky had been used solely for blending as it still is in the case of some distilleries today, although the better-known Highland malt whiskies have always had a consumer market of their own, now steadily increasing.

In 1933, when the Pot-Still Malt Distillers Association of Scotland recommended to its members that there should be no distilling that year, The Glenlivet distillery continued to work with an assured market for its output. It was then, almost unbelievably, one of only fifteen distilleries in the whole of Scotland still working, many of them only part-time, by contrast with one hundred and fifty in 1900. By this time the D.C.L. controlled some thirty-three Highland, five Islay and five Campbeltown pot-still malt distilleries, but even massive amalgamation of this nature was no cure for the malaise which affected the whisky industry, more especially when many of these distilleries were simply closed down to prevent over-production.

This was the industry's lowest point, close to complete breakdown, and the lesson was plain. High taxation had put whisky out of reach of the home market and caused overseas governments to follow suit with similar results abroad. Only the re-opening of the American market saved the day. From that year onwards the trend of exports was steadily upwards, but excessive taxation had brought the industry to the verge of collapse.

With the repeal of Prohibition there were certain difficulties at first regarding the importation of blended whisky. Fortunately Mr. Harry Lourie, the executive secretary of the National Association of Alcoholic Beverage Importers, on whom a great deal of the work devolved, was a man with an able grasp of detail. Initially there were echoes of the 'What is Whisky?' case regarding blended whisky, but this and other difficulties were overcome smoothly largely due to his efficiency and real ability. (On his retirement in 1961 he was awarded the O.B.E. and the Scotch Whisky Association made it plain how much they had appreciated his valuable service to mutual understanding and co-operation.)

In 1930 the Canadian firm of Hiram Walker, distillers in Ontario since 1858, made its first venture into the Scotch whisky industry by acquiring a controlling interest in the Stirling Bonding Co., Ltd., and a firm of blenders and importers. In 1936 they acquired Ballantine & Co., Ltd., and two Highland malt distilleries, Glenburgie and Milton Duff. Finding grain whisky in short supply, they then built a large grain distillery at Dumbarton at a cost of £3,000,000 in 1938, thus challenging the monopoly of the D.C.L., although in the words of the chairman of Hiram Walker this was nothing more than 'a development which corrects a situation in the industry which in the long run we believe could not have been for its ultimate benefit'.

It was not so much the monopoly of the D.C.L. combine which affected the industry adversely as the attitude of mind in the south. From the mid-Victorian period through to the 1930s the centralisation of power in London as the 'hub of the Empire' had resulted in Scotland being relegated in the minds of those in Whitehall and Westminster to a comfortable limbo. Too often regarded merely as a place for a sporting break in the summer or autumn recess, or as a misty, mountainous land of tartans, bagpipes and Highland Games, it is doubtful if many of the southern administrators knew the difference between a pot or patent still, however much they might enjoy the product. As a proud and independent country Scotland had ceased to exist, though possibly regarded as a 'bit of a problem' when there were severe strikes amongst unemployed shipyard-workers on the Clyde, or amongst the miners in the pits of Lanarkshire or Fife.

It was unfortunate that Lloyd George, as Chancellor and Prime Minister, was politically opposed to the drink trade and increased taxation despite his liking for whisky. Ramsay Macdonald, although Scots, was in many ways extraordinarily ignorant about his own country and viewed the distillers as capitalists from the angle of the 'class war'. Baldwin specialised in 'laissez-faire' and Neville Chamberlain, narrow in outlook like his brother, saw whisky only as something to be taxed. It is indeed significant that it was under his government in 1939 that the duty was raised once more by 10s to 82s 6d per proof gallon and again in 1940 by a further 15s to 97s 6d.

Around the end of 1938 there were several instances of prosecutions under the Merchandise Marks Act of firms attempting to sell whisky described as Scotch whisky which contained a mixture of Irish whiskey. The decision of the courts was that this was an offence at law. When the case was taken further to the Court of Appeal in Edinburgh the decision was upheld. 'Scotch whisky' meant whisky which in its entirety was distilled in Scotland. Geographically Scotch could be distilled nowhere else.

After the outbreak of the 1939 war, distilling was restricted in 1940. Due to lack of imported maize, patent-still distilling was prohibited, but limited pot-still distilling was permitted in 1940 and 1941. Thereafter, with the U-boat blockade tightening its grip, no distilling was permitted and until the year 1944–45 distilling was completely banned. Throughout the six years of war the total output distilled was less than a single year pre-war.

In 1942 the Whisky Association was dissolved on the grounds that it contained no provision within its rules for alteration. The Scotch Whisky Association was founded in its place. The objects of the new Association were stated as being:

a. to protect and promote the interests of the Scotch whisky trade generally both at home and abroad and to do all such things and to take all such measures as may be conducive or incidental to the attainment of such objects.

b. to protect the interests of owners of proprietary brands of Scotch whisky by taking such steps as the Association may think fit to regulate prices, both wholesale and retail, and to prevent such proprietary brands being sold either wholesale or retail at prices above those fixed by the Association.

In 1942 there was a further rise in duty by 40s to a total of 137s 6d per proof gallon and in the following year there was yet another rise of 20s to 157s 6d. Despite this, owing to the acute shortage of whisky, the price on the 'black market' continued to rise and the Scotch Whisky Association was at times reduced to buying up quantities of Scotch to keep the price down. Finally, during the year 1944–45, restricted pot-still malt distilling was allowed once more. Despite the restrictions involved, it appeared as if this was a first glimpse of a return to normality. The truth, however, was made plain in a minute written by Winston Churchill in April 1945 in the closing stages of the war in Europe. It read:

On no account reduce the barley for Whisky. This takes years to mature, and is an invaluable export and dollar producer. Having regard to all our other difficulties about exports, it would be most improvident not to preserve this characteristic British element of ascendency.

In 1947, under the Labour government with Hugh Dalton as Chancellor of the Exchequer, a further rise in taxation was announced, by 33s 4d to 190s 10d. Despite this unexpected and uncalled-for rise, the following year Stafford Cripps, his successor as Chancellor, added yet another 20s, making the total a round sum of £10 10s 10d per proof gallon. Forgetful, or ignorant, of the obvious fact that high taxes at home inevitably resulted in high taxes abroad, they continued to tax their most valuable asset, at the same time only allowing licences to distil for export purposes.

In 1949 full-scale distilling was allowed once more, although government restrictions still continued. Henry Ross, son of William Ross, chairman of the D.C.L. and the Scotch Whisky Association (for which he was knighted in 1952), pointed out:

. . . the present high rate of duty is indirectly responsible in our opinion for the raising of duties on Scotch whisky in many of our export markets.

When such increases in duty take place in foreign countries . . . we find that any arguments put forward to the foreign Government responsible are countered by a reply that the new rate of duty to be charged is still substantially less than that which is applicable in our own country.

It was not until 1953 that the government system of rationing supplies of grain to the distillers was finally ended. The following year they were permitted freedom of choice regarding their own export markets. For the first time since the outbreak of war in 1939 the industry was freed from all restrictions. The boom which had been slowly developing began to become a reality, but the home market had largely disappeared due to increased prices consequent on the massive rate of duty and also to lack of supplies.

One of the incidental results of tighter control following the wartime and post-war restrictions was a reduction in the overall number of Customs and Excise officers required in the service. Compared with pre-war, their ranks were considerably reduced. Apart from the closure of several distilleries, a combination of bonded warehouses and more efficient working in the distilleries themselves had helped to cut down the numbers required. Nor was there any longer any serious problem concerning illicit distillation in the Highlands. In the post-war years this was more likely to occur in the industrial cities in the English Midlands than in Scotland.

The old daily system of 'dramsirs', as they were termed, passed out to distillery workers had also largely disappeared with more efficient and tighter control within the distilleries. Yet scarcely surprisingly many of the workers managed to find a way round such bans. A favourite story concerns the resourceful worker who was walking across the yard of a Highland distillery shortly after the war with a bucket of spirit for his colleagues when to his horror he saw the Excise officer approaching. With great presence of mind he placed the bucket under the nose of a draught horse standing in the yard and returned for it later when the coast was clear. No doubt even today the distillery workers occasionally find a way to obtain a surreptitious dram, although it is no longer such a common occurrence as in the past.

A feature of the 1950s was the increasing number of American firms entering the Scotch whisky industry. Taking full advantage of the government grants offered to any overseas firm wishing to set up an industry in a development area, several distilleries were built. Thus the industry found itself in the absurd position of facing an influx of fresh competition financed in a large part by their own government. In 1950 Seagram's took over Strathisla distillery; in 1956 Seager Evans was bought by Schenley Industries of New York; in 1959 Inver House, an American-owned company, built a grain distillery near Airdrie and an associated Lowland malt distillery named Glenflagler. Both of these latter investments were in part financed by British government subsidies.

In 1960 the Scotch Whisky Association, which had been involved in legal action in France in 1958 and had been ruled out of order as a non-corporate body, decided to incorporate itself as a result. Its stated objects are: to protect and promote the interests of the industry at home and abroad; to originate, promote, support, or oppose legislative or other measures directly or indirectly affecting the industry; to enter into legal proceedings in any part of the world in defence of the interests of the industry; to collect statistical and other information relating to the industry and to supply members with such information.

With such a watchdog and with the powerful D.C.L. combine (which owns thirty-eight per cent of the industry as well as outside interests) behind the scenes, the Scotch whisky industry should be reasonably safe from outside pressure. Yet it is never easy to resist governmental pressures. Despite often repeated warnings and the obvious dangers involved, the government continued its policy of constant tax rises throughout the 1960s. The industry itself reacted in self protection in the only way open to it by larger groupings and amalgamations. The D.C.L. had set the example earlier in the century, but now seemed incapable of swaying the government's actions, admittedly no easy task. In 1968 the tax finally reached a grand total of £18 18s 6d per proof gallon.

With the 1970s came first of all decimalisation of the currency in 1971, followed by entry into the European Economic Community, the Common Market, in 1973. The discovery of North Sea Oil provided Scotland with yet another growth industry. Tourism, steadily increasing throughout the 1960s, also showed spectacular increases in the early 1970s. Combined with the Scotch whisky industry, they turned Scotland from England's poor relation into a wealthy neighbour. Increasing demands for devolution of some degree of power from London are inevitable and in accord with the increasing regionalisation taking place throughout the United Kingdom.

One of the features of the Scotch whisky industry, as has been shown, is that it is an integral part of Scotland's history and of Scotland's countryside. The pagoda-like towers of the whisky distillery maltings are a feature that may be seen throughout Scotland. Already many distilleries have opened their doors to the public and a well-worn tourist 'Whisky Trail' has been instituted on Speyside. The combination of tourism and whisky is bound to be a good one and profitable for all concerned.

It is not widely appreciated that in the past fifteen years there has been an average annual increase in exports of Scotch whisky of 11 %. Over the same period the total value of exports has increased from £56 million to £259 million in 1973. Such a fantastically profitable industry cannot be allowed to founder by fumbling of negotiations inside the European Economic Community. The whisky industry requires the right to purchase cereals at world market prices, as well as unrestricted freedom to purchase imported cereals and freedom from artificially created competition. Nor can any regulation within the E.E.C. involving partial control over the production of alcohol be allowed to affect the industry. However tough the bargaining, these must be the conditions our negotiators set in Europe or the industry is bound to be adversely affected.

In Europe and America, as at home, a noticeable feature over the past decade or more has also been the steadily growing popularity of straight malt whisky, the original Scotch, twice distilled in the pot-still in the time-honoured manner. Each distillery still produces a whisky with a subtly different flavour from its neighbour, even if they appear identical in every feature, a mystery even yet not clearly understood, despite the marvels of modern science. The combination of Scotland's barley, her peat and pure air and water, along with the skill of

Scots distillers cannot be imitated elsewhere in the world. The original Scotch, the basis of all Scotch blends, remains essentially a product of Scotland.

In this connection a notable amalgamation in 1952 was between the privately owned firms of George and J. G. Smith, Ltd., and J. & J. Grant Glen Grant, Ltd., who together formed The Glenlivet and Glen Grant Distilleries Limited, a public company. In 1970 a further merger took place with Hill Thomson & Co., Ltd., and Longmorn-Glenlivet Distilleries, Ltd. In 1972 the name of the Company so formed, by the mergers of the oldest malt distillers and the oldest merchants and blenders, was rationalised to The Glenlivet Distillers Limited. In 1974 The Glenlivet celebrated the one hundred and fiftieth anniversary of the grant of a licence to George Smith. There is now another distillery recently erected in Glenlivet, but there has been before. Come what may, in Europe or elsewhere in the world, The Glenlivet remains uniquely The Original Scotch.

Chronological Historical Outline and List of Distillers

800 B.C.	Arrack known to have been distilled in India
384 B.C.	Aristotle born; later wrote of distilling in his *Meteorology*
432 A.D.	St. Patrick, a native of Scotland, sent to Wicklow to spread Christianity and also reputed to have introduced distilling
560 A.D.	(*circa*) Taliessin the Welsh bard composed his *Song to Ale*
1263	Battle of Largs. Norwegians defeated by Scots
1314	Battle of Bannockburn. Declaration of Arbroath
1488	James III assassinated after the Battle of Sauchieburn. James IV aged 18 succeeded him. Achieved first steps towards peace with England, but Scotland orientated towards France and 'auld alliance'
1494	Entry in Exchequer Rolls regarding Friar Cor making aqua vitae by order of the King
1498	Lord High Treasurer's Account 'To the barbour that brocht aqua vitae to the King in Dundee'
1502	'Treaty of Perpetual Peace' with England
1503	James married Henry VII's eldest daughter, Margaret Tudor
1505	Barber surgeons in Edinburgh granted right of making aqua vitae
1506	Treasurer's Accounts in Inverness mention 'aqua vite to the King'
1513	James IV killed at Flodden. Succeeded by James V aged eighteen months
1523	England invaded Scotland and ravaged Jedburgh and Kelso
1527	*The vertuose boke of Distyllacyon* by Hieronymous Braunschweig published in English, translated by L. Andrew. First book on the subject, treated aqua vitae as a medicine
1539	Dissolution of the monasteries

1542	English invaded and burned Jedburgh and Kelso. James defeated at Moss. Died seven days after birth of daughter Mary, future Queen of Scots.
1544	Henry VIII's policy of 'rough wooing': invaded and burned Edinburgh and Leith, to effect marriage of infant Mary to son Edward
1545	The English burned Dryburgh, Melrose and Kelso, continuing policy
1547	The English invaded and defeated Scots at Battle of Pinkie or Musselburgh Fields, despite Henry VIII's death
1555	The Scottish Parliament passed an Act forbidding export of victuals in time of famine, except: 'It sal be leifful to the inhabitants of the burrowis of Air, Irvin, Glasgow, Dumbertane and uthers our Soverane Ladys leigis dwelland at the west setis to have bakin breid, browin aill and aqua vite to the Ilis to bertour with uther merchandice'
1559	*Treasure of Evonymous* published by Peter Morwyng, detailing methods of distilling process
1561	Mary returned from France to take up the Scottish crown
1566	Mary married Darnley and gave birth to a son, James
1567	After Darnley's murder and her abduction and marriage to Bothwell Mary was compelled to abdicate in James's favour. He was then crowned James VI of Scotland aged just over one year
1568	Defeated at Langside, Mary fled to England and was imprisoned
1578	Raphael Holinshed's *Chronicles of England, Scotland and Ireland* mention types of aqua vitae found in Scotland
1579	First Act in Scotland specifically relating to aqua vitae
1587	Mary executed at Fotheringhay
1588	The Armada defeated and wrecked
1603	The death of Queen Elizabeth and Union of the Crowns. James VI of Scotland crowned James I of England
1605	Fynes Moryson's *Itineraries* on Scotland comments on strong ale and lack of inns
1609	Statutes of Icolmkill or Iona
1616	'Act agens the drinking of Wynes in the Yllis'
1618	John Taylor in his *Pennyless Pilgrimage* visits Earl of Mar and drinks aqua vitae
	Earliest reference to 'uisge' being drunk at Highland chief's funeral
1625	James I died, succeeded by son Charles I
1636	The Worshipful Company of Distillers granted a Charter in England, the regulations framed by Sir Theodore de Mayerne and Dr. Thomas Cademan
1638	The National Covenant signed in Edinburgh
1639	The first Bishops' War: Covenanters versus Charles I

1640	The second Bishops' War: Covenanters versus Charles I
1641	Tonnage and Poundage Act in England
1642	Civil War in England: Parliament versus the Royalists
1644	The Solemn League and Covenant. The Covenanters joined Parliament against the Royalists. Imposed first Excise duty
	Following Parliament's example Charles passed an Act of Excyse on 'everie pynt of aquavytie or strong watteris sold within the country'
	Montrose raised a Highland force and was brilliantly successful
1645	After crushing all opposition Montrose was defeated at Philiphaugh
1648	Second Civil War: Cromwell versus Parliament
1649	Charles I beheaded. Scots proclaimed Charles II
	Montrose executed. Charles signed Covenant
	Cromwell invaded Scotland
1650	Battle of Dunbar. Defeat of Scots
1653	Cromwell Protector of Commonwealth
1654	Commercial Treaty signed with Portugal
1655	Excise duty in Scotland reduced
	Kirk Session records of St. Ninian's: R. Hage accused of distilling on the Sabbath
1658	Cromwell died
1660	Charles II succeeded to crown
	End to free trade between Scotland and England
1666	Pentland Rising
1673	Petition to prohibit import of brandy presented to English Parliament
1675	Boyle re-discovered the principle of the hydrometer
1678	Highland host sent to Ayrshire
1679	The battles of Drumclog and Bothwell Bridge
1685	Charles died, succeeded by James II and VII
1688	The Revolution
	An Act referred for first time to single and double proof spirits. The first attempt to charge duty according to strength
	William and Mary accepted the throne on the flight of James
1689	Dundee mortally wounded at Killiecrankie. Battle of Dunkeld
1690	Forbes of Culloden who had 'suffered the loss of his brewery of aqua vitae by fire in his absence' (in 1689) granted freedom from excise on annual payment of 400 Scots merks. Ferintosh first distillery mentioned by name
	Battle of Haughs of Cromdale ended rising in Highlands
	In England an act passed allowing anyone to distil home-grown corn
1692	The Massacre of Glencoe led to deep distrust of English in Highlands

1695	Martin Martin wrote *Description of the Western Isles of Scotland*
1698	Darien disaster promoted by William Paterson caused distrust of English by Scots and resulted in financial ruin for many Scots
1702	Anne succeeded to throne on death of William
1707	The Treaty of Union passed amid considerable dissension
1713	Treaty of Utrecht ended war in Europe
	Attempt to introduce Malt Tax in Scotland, but withdrawn
1715	Earl of Mar raised Jacobite standard in Braemar. Battle of Sheriffmuir
1725	Disarming Act in Highlands
	Walpole proposed tax on malt in Scotland. Malt Tax riots in Glasgow. Captain Bushell fired on mob. Provost Miller imprisoned by Wade, then freed on bail
1726	Captain Burt's *Letters*
1727	George II succeeded on death of George I
1736	Porteous Riots in Edinburgh result of capture of smugglers Wilson and Robertson. Escape of Robertson arranged by Wilson, who was hanged. Mob fired on by Porteous in command of troops. Porteous lynched by mob subsequently when about to be reprieved
	Scottish discontent with Union still strong, but drift southwards noticeable
	Smuggling very common and Excise officers mainly English and disliked
	Magistrates of Middlesex petitioned Parliament regarding gin
	Gin Act aimed at preventing consumption caused open flouting of law; Scotland specifically exempted from its provisions
1745	Prince Charles raised his standard at Glenfinnan. Defeated Cope at Prestonpans
1746	Battle of Falkirk. Culloden. Charles escaped via west of Scotland
1747	Intensive disarming in Highlands. 'Butcher' Cumberland earned his title after Culloden, but very repressive measures followed. Fear of Highlanders intense in south
	Efforts to 'root out Erse language' continued from days of James I and VI
	John Gow slipped over hills to Tomintoul and changed name to Smith
	Lt. Colonel Watson, C.O. Fort Augustus, advised officers to get the Highlanders 'drunk with whisky'
1750	Final Gin Act reduced the enormous consumption of gin in the south
	During the Gin Era consumption had risen from 800,000 gallons in 1694 to over 6 million gallons in 1734. By 1750 over 8 million gallons. By 1758 had dropped to 2 million gallons
1751	Act amending laws on spirits specifically ended Scotland's exemption, so that it was no longer advantageous to import from Scotland

1760   George II died, succeeded by grandson George III
1762   Admiral Sir John Lockhart introduced sheep on his Highland estate
1763   Wilkes Riots. Anti-Scots feeling very strong in England
1773   Johnson on Tour of Highlands with Boswell, had to be persuaded he would not require pistols. Visited Western Isles. Sampled usquebaugh
1784   Wash Act defined Highland Line by Act of Parliament
        Forbes's exemption at Ferintosh was finally ended
        Riots at Mr. Haig's distillery at Leith. One rioter shot and killed
        Colonel Thomas Thornton, Yorkshire sporting squire, toured Scotland
1786   Distillery Act. Licensing system introduced. Duty raised in Scotland to English level. No distinction between Highlands and Lowlands
        Unfair system gave great impetus to illicit distillation
1787   Clarke's hydrometer replaced Boyle's, but still inaccurate test
1788   Duty increased. Stein brothers bankrupted
        Robert Burns joined the Excise
        Scots distillers still continued to produce more than estimated
1789   French Revolution
1790   *First Statistical Account of Scotland* begun
1793   Outbreak of war with France
        Tax on whisky trebled to £9. Still the distillers continued to produce more whisky than had been estimated by tax officials
        William Hill set up in Rose Street, Edinburgh, as a whisky merchant
1795   Tax on whisky doubled to £18. Some stills operating continuously to beat tax at expense of wearing out still. Shape changing for sake of speed
1797   Tax trebled to £54
1798   Committee on Distilleries set up to investigate
1799   Malcolm Gillespie joined the Excise
1800   Dr. John Leyden's *Tour to the Highlands*
        Tax doubled yet again to £108
1802   Treaty of Amiens resulted in temporary peace
1803   War broke out again and tax raised yet again to £162
        Between 1740 and 1815 86 Highland regiments were embodied
        The introduction of sheep and the resulting Clearances from 1760s onwards began to empty the Highlands; by mid-19th century all these processes had reached their natural conclusion. Meanwhile whisky was becoming the most important industry. Illicit distilling was accepted by everyone as the only means of paying rent for a farm. The taxation problem had clearly defeated the government in the south
1805   The firm of Seager Evans was formed in London as makers of gin

1812	Colonel Peter Hawker visited Scotland, saw signs of smuggling
1814	The prohibition of stills under 500 gallon capacity in the Highlands; according to General Stewart of Garth this amounted to a complete interdict
	Matthew Gloag set up as a whisky merchant in Perth
1815	Waterloo finally ended Napoleon's power. Peace returned to Europe
	The output of the distillery at Drumin in Glenlivet run by George Smith, grandson of John Smith Gow, was already a hogshead a week. Due to the pure water and fine peat available the whisky in Glenlivet was famed as being the finest illicit whisky in the Highlands. It was drunk by many northern lairds, including Grant of Rothiemurchos, M.P. and lawyer
	Laphroaig distillery on Islay was built by the Johnstone family
1817	Teaninich distillery built by Captain H. Munro in Ross-shire
	Sikes's hydrometer superseded the old inaccurate Clarke's hydrometer
1818	Bladnoch distillery was founded, near Wigtown, by the Maclelland family
1819	Clyneleish distillery near Brora was built by the Marquis of Stafford, son of the Duke of Sutherland
1820	John Walker set up as a licensed grocer in Kilmarnock in Ayrshire
	Debates in Parliament on the subject of illicit distilling in Scotland were inconclusive, but the Duke of Gordon addressed the House of Lords urging a more moderate policy
	George III died, succeeded by George IV
	Sikes's hydrometer and saccharometer used in conjunction under new Act
1821	Linkwood distillery near Elgin was built
1822	George IV visited Scotland and was provided with illicit Glenlivet whisky by Grant of Rothiemurchos. He was reported to drink no other
	General David Stewart of Garth wrote his *Sketches of the Character, Manners and Present State of the Highlanders of Scotland*
1823	A new Act was introduced which provided for a £10 annual licence fee and a duty of 2s 3d per gallon
	Springbank distillery near Campbeltown founded by farmers named Mitchell
1824	Under the aegis of his landlord the Duke of Richmond and Gordon, farmer and illicit distiller George Smith was the first to take out a licence under the new Act. The first legal distillery in Glenlivet, his neighbours threatened to burn it down
	Gillespie made a notable haul of illicit Glenlivet whisky in a desperate battle with smugglers. Gillespie then applied for a less arduous post
1825	Consolidation Act introduced uniform measures
	T. R. Sandeman founded a whisky merchant's business in Perth

1826   Robert Stein took out a patent for a single-distillation still
Tax raised to 2s 10d per proof gallon

1827   Gillespie forged a bill, was arrested, tried and hanged, despite pleas for mercy on account of his long service
Christopher North's *Noctes Ambrosianae* featured James Hogg in *Blackwood's Magazine*

1830   Tax per proof gallon raised to 3s 6d. Consequent increase in smuggling
Stein built his first still at Kirkliston, a Haig distillery
William Teacher founded his merchant's firm, aged 19
Talisker distillery was founded on the Isle of Skye

1831   Aeneas Coffey invented his single still, known as the patent Coffey still, providing continuous distillation for grain whisky
Justerini and Brooks founded their partnership in London

1832   The Coffey still was patented and approved
The Glen Scotia distillery founded in Campbeltown by Stewart Galbraith
Total abstinence was advocated at the Preston Temperance meeting

1833   The Parnell Commission of Enquiry into the Liquor Trade started

1836   The Parnell Commission issued its findings. Mostly ineffectual
The Glenfarclas Glenlivet distillery was founded by Robert Hay

1837   Queen Victoria came to the throne

1838   Hill Thomson granted Royal Warrant

1840   The Glen Grant distillery was founded at Rothes by James and John Grant
The Glenkinchie distillery in East Lothian founded by farmer J. Gray
The tax per proof gallon was raised to 3s 8d

1841   James Chivas founded his firm of merchants and grocers in Aberdeen

1842   Glenmorangie distillery at Tain was founded by William Mathieson

1846   John Dewar started as a wine and spirit merchant in Perth
The Repeal of the Corn Laws was to affect grain distilling favourably

1848   Queen Victoria and family visited John Begg's distillery at Lochnagar

1849   Captain William Grant announced his distillery in conjunction with George Smith's at Drumin the only ones in Glenlivet

1853   Andrew Usher was credited with producing the first blended whisky
Tax raised by Gladstone to 4s 8d per proof gallon

1854   Outbreak of the Crimean War. Tax raised to 6s per proof gallon

1855   Tax raised to 8s per proof gallon

1856   First Trade Arrangement amongst grain distillers
End of Crimean War
Tax raised a further 1d per proof gallon

1857   W. & A. Gilbey founded as wine and spirit merchants

	William Thomson joined William Hill and formed Hill Thomson at 45, Frederick Street, Edinburgh
1860	Gladstone raised the duty to 10s per proof gallon
1865	New Trade Arrangement formed. Menzies, Barnard & Craig, John Bald & Co., John Haig & Co., MacNab Bros, Robert Mowbray and Macfarlane & Co., who replaced John Crabbie and Co., who had previously been a member
	Glenfarclas distillery was bought by John Grant of Blairfindy
1870	*Phylloxera vastatrix* beginning to spread in France
1874	The North of Scotland Malt Distillers Association was formed
1877	The Distillers Company Limited was formed by Macfarlane & Co., John Bald & Co., John Haig & Co., MacNab Bros & Co., Robert Mowbray and Stewart & Co.
	John Haig founded his company at Markinch in Fife
1880	John Walker opened a London office
	Colonel John Gordon Smith, son of George Smith, went to law on the subject of the use of the name Glenlivet. The court held he was the only one entitled to use the label 'The Glenlivet', all others had to use a prefix
1881	Bruichladdich Islay Malt distillery was founded
1882	William Sanderson produced his blend 'Vat 69'
	James Whyte and Charles Mackay founded Whyte and Mackay, Ltd.
1884	James Buchanan set up in London and produced the blend 'Black & White'
	William Shaw joined Hill Thomson and produced the blend 'Queen Anne'
1885	Gladstone defeated on proposed tax
1886	The D.C.L. shares were finally quoted on the London Stock Exchange
1887	The Glenfiddich distillery was built by William Grant
	The Dufftown-Glenlivet distillery was founded
	Highland Distilleries founded to acquire the Islay distillery of William Grant and the Glenrothes Glenlivet Distillery built in 1878
1888	The North British Distillery Co. with productive capacity of three million gallons p.a. founded in opposition to the growing power of the D.C.L.
	Mackie & Co. took over Lagavulin distillery on Islay for White Horse
1890	The Playfair Parliamentary Commission formed under Sir Lyon Playfair
1891	Balvenie distillery founded by William Grant of Glenfiddich
1893	Cardow was bought by John Walker
	The firm of Macdonald and Muir was founded
1894	Longmorn-Glenlivet built by Longmorn Co.
1895	Aultmore founded by Alexander Edward of Sanquhar, Forres
	Arthur Bell & Sons formed from Sandeman's of Perth
1896	John Dewar built a distillery at Aberfeldy

1898	The whisky boom came to an abrupt halt with the failure of the Pattison brothers
1899	The United Yeast Co. was founded by the D.C.L. as a subsidiary
	The Boer War broke out in South Africa
1900	Tax per proof gallon raised to 11s
1901	Queen Victoria died, succeeded by Edward VII
1902	The Boer War ended
1906	Islington Borough Council brought the 'What is Whisky?' case. Basically a question of malt versus grain. Verdict in magistrate's court in favour of malt, but the D.C.L. pressed for Royal Commission
1908	A Royal Commission on Whisky decided grain and malt blended to make Scotch whisky
1909	Lloyd George raised the tax per proof gallon to 14s 9d
1910	Edward VII died, succeeded by George V
1914	The First World War
	Intoxicating Liquor Act
	Scottish Malt Distillers formed as a subsidiary of the D.C.L.
1915	Central Liquor Control Board formed
	Immature Spirits Act required two years' compulsory bonding
	Buchanan's and Dewars merged into Buchanan-Dewars
1916	Compulsory bonding extended to three years
1917	Dilution of proof to 30 under proof
	Whisky Association formed
1918	Tax per proof gallon increased by 15s 3d to 30s, by Bonar Law
	War ended
1919	Austen Chamberlain increased tax per proof gallon by 20s to 50s
	Haig and Haig were taken over by the D.C.L.
1920	Prohibition was introduced in the U.S.A.
	Chamberlain increased the tax to 72s 6d per proof gallon
	The post-war boom ended
1924	John Haig merged with the D.C.L.
1925	Buchanan-Dewars and John Walker merged with the D.C.L., with John Ross of the D.C.L. as chairman
1926	The Pot-Still Malt Distillers Association was formed in place of the North of Scotland Malt Distillers Association to include all malt distillers
1927	Seager Evans set up Strathclyde distillery for grain whisky
	White Horse Distillers was acquired by the D.C.L.
1928	The Distillers Co. of Canada took over Seagram and Sons
1929	The Wall Street crash. Slump followed

1930	Hiram Walker of Ontario acquired Glenburgie-Glenlivet
1932	Prohibition was repealed by President F. D. Roosevelt
1933	Arthur Bell & Sons acquired Blair Athol and Dufftown-Glenlivet distilleries
1936	Hiram Walker acquired George Ballantine & Co. of Dumbarton, also Milton Duff distillery
	George V died, succeeded by Edward VIII who abdicated; succeeded in turn by George VI
	Arthur Bell & Sons acquired the Inchgower distillery near Fochabers
	Seager Evans acquired John Long
1937	Seager Evans took over Glenugie distillery at Peterhead, Aberdeenshire
1938	Hiram Walker opened a £3,000,000 grain distillery at Inverleven, Dumbarton
1939	Outbreak of Second World War
	Tax per proof gallon raised by 10s to 82s 6d
	Total whisky stocks lost by enemy action amounted to 4½ million gallons
	Grain distilling halted, limited malt pot-still distilling allowed
1940	Tax per proof gallon raised by 15s to 97s 6d
1942	Tax per proof gallon raised by 40s to 137s 6d
	The Whisky Association dissolved and The Scotch Whisky Association founded in its place
1943	Tax per proof gallon raised by 20s to 157s 6d
1945	End of Second World War
1947	Distilling still greatly restricted
	Tax per proof gallon raised by 33s 4d to 190s 10d. Hugh Dalton Chancellor of Exchequer
1948	Stafford Cripps raised tax per proof gallon by 20s to 210s 10d
1950	Seagram's took over Strathisla distillery
1952	George VI died, succeeded by Elizabeth II
	George & J. G. Smith, Ltd. and J. & J. Grant Glen Grant, Ltd. formed a public company, The Glenlivet & Glen Grant Distillers, Ltd.
1954	Hiram Walker took over Glencadam distillery in Brechin and the Scapa distillery in Orkney
1955	Hiram Walker took over Pulteney distillery in Wick
1956	Seager Evans were bought by Schenley Industries of New York, in turn owned by Glen Alden Corporation
1957	Seager Evans built Kinclaith distillery near Glasgow
1958	Seager Evans built a new distillery at Tormore on the Spey, north of Grantown
1959	Inver House, an American-owned Company, built a new grain distillery by

	Airdrie and an associated Lowland malt distillery named Glenflagler
1960	The Scotch Whisky Association was incorporated to provide legal status in foreign courts
	Glenfarclas distillery redoubled in size
	Ledaig distillery in Tobermory started
	Jura distillery started by Scottish & Newcastle Breweries, Ltd.
	Glenallachie distillery started
1961	The tax per proof gallon was raised by 21s to 231s 10d
1962	Laphroaig was acquired by Seager Evans
	W. & A. Gilbey, Gilbey Twiss, Justerini & Brooks and United Vintners formed International Distillers and Vintners, Ltd.
1964	The tax per proof gallon was raised to £12.87
1965	The tax per proof gallon was raised to £14.60
	Caperdonich and Benriach distilleries were re-built after having been silent for over sixty years
	Invergordon Distillers, Ltd., was formed
1966	The tax per proof gallon was raised to £16.06
1968	The tax per proof gallon was raised to £17.14 in March. In November it was raised again to £18.85
1969	Glen Alden Corporation who owned Schenley Industries who owned Seager Evans was taken over by Rapid American Incorporated. The name Seager Evans was changed to Long John International, Ltd.
1970	The Glenlivet & Glen Grant Distilleries, Ltd., merged with Hill Thomson & Co., Ltd., and Longmorn-Glenlivet Distilleries, Ltd.
	Amalgamated Distilled Products, Ltd., was formed with the Campbeltown Glen Scotia distillery and other interests
	The Highland Distillers Co., Ltd., acquired Matthew Gloag, Ltd.
1971	Chivas Bros., the Scots subsidiary of Seagrams, began plans for a distillery in Glenlivet
	Decimalisation of currency in Britain
1972	The Glenlivet & Glen Grant Distilleries, Ltd., rationalised their name to The Glenlivet Distillers Limited
	The Pot-Still Malt Distillers Association of Scotland rationalised their name to The Malt Distillers Association of Scotland
1973	Britain entered the European Economic Community
	With the introduction of V.A.T. the duty on whisky was reduced for the first time since 1896
	Dalmore, Whyte & Mackay and Tomintoul distillery taken over by The House of Fraser

Braes of Glenlivet distillery operational

The notable feature of the late fifties and sixties has been the influx of foreign, particularly U.S., investment in the industry, taking full advantage of government subsidies but not necessarily with the interests of the industry or of the United Kingdom at heart

1974   The Glenlivet Distillers Ltd. celebrate their hundred and fiftieth anniversary since George Smith took out the first licence in 1824

Malt Distillers of Scotland celebrate their centenary

As at 1974 there are the following distillers with their distilleries and chief blends:

Aberlour-Glenlivet Distillery Company.
   Distillery: Aberlour-Glenlivet.
Ardbeg Distillery Company.
   Distillery: Ardbeg.
Amalgamated Distilled Products.
   Distillery: Glen Scotia.
Barton Brands.
   Distilleries: Littlemill; Loch Lomond.
   Blend: House of Stewart.
Arthur Bell.
   Distilleries: Blair Athol; Dufftown-Glenlivet; Ichgower; Pittyvaich-Glenlivet.
   Blends: Bell's; Mackenzie; Royal Vat.
Ben Nevis Distillery Company.
   Distillery: Ben Nevis.
Chivas Brothers (a subsidiary of Joseph E. Seagram & Sons, Inc.)
   Distilleries: Glen Keith-Glenlivet; Strathisla-Glenlivet; Braes of Glenlivet.
   Blends: Chivas Regal; 100 Pipers; Passport.
Clan Munro Whisky Company.
   Distillery: Macduff.
Distillers Company.
   Distilleries: Aberfeldy; Aultmore; Balmenach; Banff; Benrinnes; Benromach; Caledonian; Cambus; Cameronbridge; Caol Ila; Cardow; Carsebridge; Clynelish; Coleburn; Convalmore; Cragganmore; Craigellachie; Dailuaine; Dallus Dhu; Dalwhinnie; Glen Albyn; Glendullan; Glen Elgin; Glenkinchie; Glenlochy; Glenlossie; Glen Mhor; Glentauchers; Glenury-Royal; Hillside; Imperial; Knockdhu; Lagavulin; Linkwood; Mannochmore; Millburn; Mortlach; North Port; Oban; Ord; Port Dundas; Port Ellen; Rosebank; Royal Brackla; Royal

Lochnager; Speyburn; St. Magdalene; Talisker; Teaninich.

Blends: Antiquary; Abbots Choice; Black and White; Bulloch Lade; Dewars; Crawfords; Haig; Haig Pinch; Harveys; King George IV; Old Parr; Ushers; Vat 69; Johnnie Walker; White Horse.

Eadie Cairns.

Distillery: Auchentoshan.

Blend: Cairns.

Glenlivet Distillers, The

Distilleries: Benriach-Glenlivet; Caperdonich; Glen Grant-Glenlivet; The Glenlivet; Longmorn-Glenlivet.

Blends: Queen Anne; Something Special; St. Leger.

Glenturret Distillery Company.

Distillery: Glenturret.

J. & G. Grant.

Distillery: Glenfarclas-Glenlivet.

William Grant.

Distilleries: Balvenie; Girvan; Glenfiddich; Ladyburn.

Blends: Standfast; Clan MacGregor.

Highland Distilleries Company.

Distilleries: Bunnahabhain; Glenglassaugh; Glenrothes-Glenlivet; Highland Park; Tamdhu-Glenlivet.

Blend: Famous Grouse.

International Distillers & Vintners.

Distilleries: Auchroisk; Glen Spey; Knockando; Strathmill.

Blend: J & B Rare; Spey Royal.

Invergordon Distillers.

Distilleries: Bruichladdich; Ben Wyvis; Deanston; Invergordon; Tamnavulin-Glenlivet; Tullibardine.

Blend: Findlaters Finest.

Inverhouse Distillers.

Distilleries: Bladnoch; Glenflagler; Moffat.

Blends: Macarthurs; Inverhouse.

Ledaig Distillery Company.

Distillery: Tobermory.

Long John International.

Distilleries: Glenugie; Kinclaith; Laphroaig; Strathclyde; Tormore.

Blends: Long John; Islay Mist.

Macallan-Glenlivet.

Distillery: Macallan-Glenlivet.

MacDonald Martin Distilleries.
> Distilleries: Glenmorangie; Glen Moray-Glenlivet.
> Blends: Martins VVO; Highland Queen; Muirheads.

MacNab.
> Distillery: Lochside.

J. A. Mitchell.
> Distillery: Springbank.

Stanley P. Morrison & Co.
> Distilleries: Bowmore; Glengarioch.

North British Distillery Company.
> Distillery: North British.

North of Scotland Distilling Company.
> Distillery: Strathmore.

Robertson & Baxter.
> Distillery: Glengoyne.
> Blends: Cutty Sark; Langs; Red Hackle.

Scottish & Newcastle Breweries.
> Distilleries: Isle of Jura; Glenallachie.
> Blends: Mackinlays; MacPhersons Cluny.

Scottish Universal Investment Trust (a subsidiary of the House of Fraser).
> Distilleries: Dalmore; Fettercairn; Tomintoul-Glenlivet.
> Blend: Whyte & Mackay Special.

Speyside Distillery Company.
> Distillery: Speyside.

Teacher (Distillers).
> Distilleries: Ardmore; Glendronach.
> Blend: Highland Cream.

Tomatin Distillers.
> Distillery: Tomatin.
> Blend: Big T.

Hiram Walker & Sons.
> Distilleries: Balblair; Dumbarton; Inverleven/Lomond; Glenburgie-Glenlivet; Glencadam; Miltonduff-Glenlivet; Pulteney; Scapa.
> Blends: Ambassador; Ballantines; Old Smuggler; Lauders.

William Whiteley.
> Distillery: Edradour.
> Blends: House of Lords; Kings Ransom.

Bibliography

Arnot, Hugo. A History of Edinburgh. Edinburgh, 1779

Barnard, Alfred. The Whisky Distilleries of the United Kingdom. Harper, 1887

Boswell, James. Journal of a Tour of the Hebrides. London, 1956

Brander, Michael. The Life and Sport of the Inn. Gentry Books, 1973

Brander, Michael. A Guide to Scotch Whisky. Johnston & Bacon, 1974.

Brown, Peter H. History of Scotland. 3 vols. 1911

Burns, James Dawson. A History of Temperance. 2 vols. 1881–90

Burns, Robert. Complete Works. Kilmarnock edition, 1876

Burt, Captain Edward. Letters from a Gentleman in the North. 2 vols. London, 1754

Burton, John Hill. History of Scotland. 8 vols. 1873

Calder, R. H. Glenlivet Gleanings, Banff, 1924

Carlyle, Rev. Alexander. Autobiography. Edinburgh, 1860

Culloden papers. T. Cadell & Davies. London, 1815

Daiches, David. Scotch Whisky. Deutsch, 1969

Dunnett, Alastair. The Land of Scotch. S.W.A., 1953

Forbes, K. J. A Short History of the Art of Distillation. Leiden, 1948

Fyfe, J. G. (Ed.). Scottish Diaries & Memoirs. 1746–1843. Stirling, 1942

Gillespie, Malcolm, The Memorial and Case of. 1827

Glenlivet, The Annals of the Distillery. 1924, reprinted 1959

Graham, H. G. The Social Life of Scotland in the 18th Century. Black, 1950

Grant, Elizabeth, of Rothiemurchos. Memoirs of a Highland Lady 1797–1827. **Ed.** Angus Davidson. John Murray. 1950

Gunn, Neil M. Whisky and Scotland. Routledge, 1935

Morrison, Brian. Drink and the Victorians, 1971

Hawker, Colonel Peter. Diaries. 1782–1851

Kinross, Lord. The Kindred Spirit. Newman Neame, 1959

Laing, Andrew. History of Scotland. 4 vols. 1900–6

Laver, James. The House of Haig. 1958

Leyden, Dr. J. Journal of a Tour to the Highlands in 1800. Edinburgh, 1805

Lockhart, Sir Robert Bruce. Scotch. Putnam, 1959

MacDonald, Aeneas. Whisky. The Porpoise Press, 1930

MacDonald, Ian. Smuggling in the Highlands. Inverness, 1914

Mackenzie, Osgood. A Hundred Years in the Highlands. Bles, 1921

Mackie, Albert D. The Scotch Whisky Drinker's Companion. Ramsay Head, 1973

MacLeod, Donald. Gloomy Memories of the Highlands. Edinburgh, 1860

Martin, Martin. Account of the Western Isles. Glasgow, 1884

McDowall, Professor R. J. S. The Whiskies of Scotland. John Murray, 1967

Menary, George (Ed.). Life and Letters of Duncan Forbes of Culloden. 1936

Miller, Hugh. My Schools and Schoolmasters. Edinburgh, 1907

Mitchell, Joseph. Reminiscences of My Life in the Highlands. 2 vols. 1883

Moryson, Fynes. Itineraries. 1605–1617

Morwyng, Peter. Treasure of Evonymous. 1559

Robb, J. Marshall. Scotch Whisky. W. & R. Chambers, 1950

Ross, James. Whisky. Routledge, 1970

St. John, Charles. Wild Sports & Natural History of the Highlands. Murray, 1893

Saintsbury, George. Notes on a Cellar Book. Macmillan, 1920

Sillett, S. W. Illicit Scotch. Beaver Books, Aberdeen, 1965

Simon, André. Drink. London, 1948

Sinclair, Sir John, Bt. Statistical Account of Scotland. 21 vols. Edinburgh, 1791–1799

Smith, C. Marshall. Strathspey Highways & Byways. Elgin, 1957

Southey, Robert. Journal of a Tour in Scotland. 1819

Stewart, Major General David, of Garth. Sketches of the Character, Manners and Present State of the Highlanders of Scotland. 2 vols. 1822

Taylor, Iain Cameron. Highland Whisky. An Comunn Caidhealach, 1968.

Taylor, John. Pennyless Pilgrimage. 1649

Thornton, Colonel Thomas. Highland Tour, 1784. London, 1805

Weir, Ronald B. History of the Pot Still Malt Distillers' Association. Elgin, 1970

Wilson, John. Scotland's Malt Whiskies. Dumbarton, 1973

Wilson, John. Christopher North: Noctes Ambrosianae. 4 vols. Edinburgh, 1860

Wilson, Ross. Scotch Made Easy. Hutchinson, 1959

Wilson, Ross. Scotch. Constable, 1970

Wilson, Ross. Scotch, Its History and Romance. David & Charles, 1973